Britain since 1945

By the same author

GEORGE ELIOT: Godless Woman
JOSEPH CONRAD: Text and Context
HOW TO STUDY A JOSEPH CONRAD NOVEL

Britain since 1960

An Introduction

BRIAN SPITTLES

MACMILLAN

First published 1995 by
MACMILLAN PRESS LTD
Houndmills, Basingstoke, Hampshire RG21 2XS
and London
Companies and representatives
throughout the world

ISBN 0–333–60783–X hardcover
ISBN 0–333–60784–8 paperback

A catalogue record for this book is available from the British Library

Printed in Malaysia

10   9   8   7   6   5   4   3   2   1
04   03   02   01   00   99   98   97   96   95

For Rod and Ann
more than relatives, good friends

Contents

Acknowledgements

A great many people have contributed either directly or indirectly to my understanding of the subjects in this book, and it is impossible to name them all. A few people, though, have been indispensable to me, and those I must thank. Although she may not wish to be associated with all the views expressed in it, the book would never have been written at all without the initial inspiration and encouragement of Professor Emma Harris. Her great energy and generosity of spirit provided the original impetus, and our discussions always took place in an atmosphere of good food, wine and fellowship at her table.

I would like to thank Joyce Alied for invaluable assistance. The library staff of the Bodleian have been superb, and particularly the three wonderful people running the Map Room, without whom my newspaper research would have been impossible. Val, Chris and David, at Ruskin College library, have been literally invaluable, collectively a vast source of information, ideas and good humour. Behind every academic who spends a lot of time writing there is some unsung hero who is actually doing the work back at the ranch. I wish to thank Dr Stephen Regan for taking up many of my college burdens, and remaining a good friend whilst doing so. Also I cannot register warmly enough in public my appreciation of my colleague Tom Sherry, who, woefully exploited as he has been, still shares a cup of coffee and a joke with me. Sylvie and Paul helped me with the films. Ian Seaton, Dick Alford and Nick Wadham-Smith of the British Council created the circumstances in which I was able to think about my native country with, I hope, some objectivity. I wish also to thank the many students I met through Ian and Dick for their inspirational help. As always, Margaret Wickett contributed most for least reward.

More generally I want to pay my respects to two men who have each profoundly helped to change my life. I read Richard Hoggart's first book when I was a very frustrated lathe operator, and he unwittingly put me on the educational road as an adult student. We often meet such people in the flesh with trepidation they'll have feet of clay, but subsequently meeting Richard Hoggart was no disappointment – indeed a great honour. The other man to change my thinking and life radically is Dr Charles Green-leaf Bell. His massive forty-two-video compilation, *Symbolic History*, is a great delight of learning to which I return as often as possible. It has also been my great honour to meet Charles Bell on many occasions: a man of immense genius, energy and charm without whose stimulus I would never have written anything.

The author and publisher wish to thank the following who have kindly given permission for the use of copyright material:

The Economist, for the extracts from various editions of *The Economist*, copyright © 1969, 1974, 1985, 1987, 1988;

Financial Times, for the extracts from various editions of the *Financial Times*;

Guardian News Services Ltd, for the extracts from *New Society and New Statesman*;

Roy Jenkins, for the extracts from his 'Richard Dimbleby Lecture', BBC 1 (1979);

Morning Star Co-operative Society Ltd, for the extracts from issues of the *Morning Star*;

News Group Newspapers Ltd, for the extracts from various issues of *The Sun*;

Solo Syndication Ltd, for the extracts from various issues of *The Daily Mail*; copyright © Solo Syndication;

Syndication International Ltd, for the extracts from various issues of the *Daily Mirror* and *Sunday Mirror*.

Every effort has been made to trace all the copyright-holders but if any have been been inadvertently overlooked the publisher will be pleased to make the necessary arrangement at the first opportunity.

NB: By-lines are given where they are printed in newspapers and journals. If no by-line is attributed, it is because none was given in the original source.

Selected Chronology

	Primarily international	Primarily political/economic	Primarily social
1942			Beveridge Report
1944			Butler Education Act
1945	Second World War ends (beginning of atomic/nuclear weapons)	Labour Party wins election with 146-seat majority Attlee becomes PM (creation of Welfare State and nationalisation of central industries follows)	
1947	Intensification of Cold War splits world into USSR/USA polarisation		
1949	Communists win civil war in China		
1950	Korean War begins	Labour Party wins election with 5-seat majority	
1951		Conservatives win election with 17-seat majority Churchill becomes PM	
1953	Korean War ends		Coronation of Elizabeth II
1955		Eden becomes PM	Commercial television begins

	Primarily international	Primarily political/economic	Primarily social
1956	Britain and France invade Suez Canal area		*Look Back in Anger* begins new phase in British theatre
	USSR invades Hungary		*Rock Around the Clock* disturbances
			Anti-Suez war demonstrations
1957	USSR launches Sputnik I	Macmillan becomes PM. 'Never had it so good' speech signals 'age of affluence' (TV sets, car ownership, foreign holidays, etc.)	CND formed
1958			First outbreak of race riots
1959		Conservatives win election with 100-seat majority	
1960			*Lady Chatterley's Lover* court case
			Female contraceptive pill developed
			Film version of *Saturday Night and Sunday Morning* starts British 'new wave'

	Primarily international	Primarily political/economic	Primarily social
1961	Berlin Wall erected First manned space flight	Britain's application for EEC membership	*A Taste of Honey* wins film awards
1962	Cuban missile crisis brings world to brink of nuclear war	Macmillan's 'night of the long knives' First Commonwealth Immigrants Act	*Lawrence of Arabia* wins film Oscars
1963	de Gaulle vetoes British membership of EEC Kennedy assassinated	Profumo and Philby sex and spy scandals Macmillan resigns; Home becomes PM	
1964		Labour Party wins election with 4-seat majority Wilson becomes PM	BBC2 TV begins
1965	USA sends combat troops into Vietnam War	Heath replaces Home as Conservative leader Southern Rhodesia UDI crisis First Race Relations Act	Capital punishment abolished
1966		Labour Party wins election with 96-seat majority Welsh Nationalists win by-election	England win football World Cup

	Primarily international	Primarily political/economic	Primarily social
1967	Kenyan Asians expelled de Gaulle vetoes British membership of EEC Nigerian civil war begins	Devaluation of sterling Scottish Nationalists win by-election	Influx of Kenyan Asian immigrants Laws on homosexuality relaxed Colour TV begins
1968	British withdrawal from 'east of Suez' begins USSR invades Czechoslovakia	Commonwealth Immigrants Act Race Relations Act	Mass demonstrations against Vietnam War
1969	USA land men on the moon	British troops sent to Northern Ireland (temporarily) Attempts to regulate trade union power begin	*In Place of Strife* Divorce laws relaxed
1970	Nigerian civil war ends	First general election at which 18–20-year-olds vote Conservatives win election with 30-seat majority Heath becomes PM Industrial Relations Act	*The Female Eunuch* First Women's Liberation conference

	Primarily international	Primarily political/economic	Primarily social
1971		Immigration Act	
1972	Ugandan Asians expelled	(London)derry 'Bloody Sunday' tragedy escalates Ulster crisis	Influx of Ugandan Asian immigrants
		Ulster Assembly abolished	*Spare Rib* begins publication
		NUM strike defeats government's pay restraint policy	
		Unemployment reaches one million	
		Parliament debates EEC membership	
1973	Arab–Israeli War	Britain joins EEC	Acute oil/petrol shortage
			Three-day working week imposed
			Minimum school-leaving age raised to 16
			Virago begins publishing

	Primarily international	Primarily political/economic	Primarily social
1974	Cyprus crisis between Turkey and Greece	NUM strike	
		No party wins an overall February election majority	
		Wilson becomes PM	
		Labour wins October election with 3-seat majority	
		Inflation reaches highest ever peak of 28%	
		IRA bombing in Birmingham	
		Local Government reorganised	
1975	Vietnam War ends	Monetarism formally replaces Keynesian economics	Commission for Equal Opportunities
		EEC membership referendum	
		Equal Pay Act	
		Sex Discrimination Act	
		Thatcher becomes Conservative leader	
1976		Wilson resigns	*The Right Approach*
		Callaghan becomes PM	
		Race Relations Act	

	Primarily international	Primarily political/economic	Primarily social
1977	Prague 'Charter 77' proclaimed for human rights		Commission for Racial Equality
1979	ERM formed	Employment Protection Act (for women)	
	First Euro-elections (subsequently held every 5 years)	'Winter of discontent' sees widespread strikes	
	USSR invades Afghanistan	Welsh and Scottish referenda reject national devolution	
		Conservatives win election with 43-seat majority	
		Thatcher becomes PM	
		Income Tax reduced	
		VAT virtually doubled	
		Thatcher causes crisis with EEC	
1980	Solidarity movement in Poland begins	Act of Parliament restricting trade unions	Bristol riots
		Foot becomes Labour Party leader	
		Southern Rhodesia crisis resolved	
1981		Social Democratic Party formed (leading to later SDP/Liberal Alliance)	Brixton and Liverpool riots

	Primarily international	Primarily political/economic	Primarily social
1982	Falklands War	Act of Parliament further restricting trade unions	Channel Four TV *Chariots of Fire* wins film Oscars
1983		Conservatives win election with 154-seat majority Kinnock becomes Labour Party leader	*Gandhi* wins film Oscars
1984		Ban on GCHQ trade unions Act of Parliament further restricting trade unions NUM strike begins IRA bomb Conservative Party Conference hotel Privatisation begins in earnest	Divorce made easier
1985		NUM defeated after year-long strike Unemployment officially reaches 3 million for first time	Widespread street riots in many major towns
1986	USA bombing reprisals against Libya	Large (Labour) Metropolitan Boroughs abolished	

	Primarily international	Primarily political/economic	Primarily social
1987		Conservatives win election with 102-seat majority	
		Stock Exchange crash	
1988		Thatcher launches virulent attack on EEC	
		Act of Parliament further restricting trade unions	
		Education Act controlling teaching	
1989	Final collapse of Soviet communism	Poll Tax begins in Scotland	
	USSR troops leave Afghanistan	SDP disintegrates	
		Liberal Democratic Party formed	
1990		Poll Tax begins in rest of Britain	Widespread Poll Tax riots
		Britain joins ERM	
		Ridley attacks EEC	
		Thatcher forced to resign	
		Major becomes PM	

	Primarily international	Primarily political/economic	Primarily social
1991	Political reunification of Germany		
	Gulf War		
	Break up of Yugoslavia in civil war		
1992	Denmark and France almost reject Maastricht Treaty	Conservatives win election with 17-seat majority	Mass protests against pit closures
	Britain withdraws from ERM	Smith becomes Labour Party leader	
		Sterling devalued	
1993	Israeli–Palestinian peace agreement	IRA Warrington bombing	Teachers confront government on education changes
	ERM collapses	Pit closures carried out	
		Maastricht Treaty narrowly and acrimoniously accepted	
		Joint London/Dublin Downing Street Declaration for Peace in Northern Ireland	
1994		VAT range extended (includes domestic fuel for first time)	
		Ulster violence continues until September ceasefire	

Introduction

History is anything that happened before you opened this book. It might be argued, from a beginner's point of view, that politics is a way of organising what is going on around you, and has been a form of organisation in society throughout history; and that sociology is one of several ways of analysing society, and society itself is surrounding you even as you read these sentences. This book is an attempt to understand the recent past and the present, which is where the past has got to so far, through the disciplines of politics, history and branches of sociology – in general, social studies, or British Studies, the study of Britain.

We often think of history as the distant past, but it is *all* the past. Historians, teachers and the older generations generally tend to consider that the period of their own life is still somehow the present. Perhaps because it is present in their own experience, it is a force that has helped to shape what they are as individuals. It is not uncommon, for example, to hear people say 'everyone can remember what they were doing when they heard the news of John F. Kennedy's assassination'. That was certainly an awful event – but the US president was killed in November 1963, and obviously anyone born since 1960, and that is now a very great many people, is not part of that 'everyone'.

That incident was not just a matter of history, its consequences affected politics too, and through that the nature of the society as it developed subsequently. The events discussed in this book are part of my experience, the politics of my life, features that shaped the society in which I live. I grew up during, and lived through, most of the events explored in this book, and as a teacher I have sometimes taken it for granted that students would know something, would understand a situation, a political, social or cultural attitude, because it was part of the personal experience of my life. I knew it without having had to study it. But there is no reason at all why a student should be expected to have such knowledge. The errors I made of that kind inspired me to write this book. Here, nothing is taken for granted.

In the film *Nothing But the Best*, a satire on the politics of social life made early in this period, a hopeful young man asks an older character's advice about how to get on in a career after leaving university. The dialogue goes (with the older character speaking first):

> If pressed you're probably best to say that you read History. You don't know any history, do you?
> No...
> Excellent![1]

The days when ignorance was an advantage in life have gone, and even politicians, sociologists and historians are required to understand something of their society now, and how it came to have the forms it has. The purpose of this book is to throw light on that, by passing on some knowledge, understanding and appreciation of the fairly recent past.

Continuity Ruptured

Any date chosen to start a book is to some extent random. 1960 has been chosen here as a round-figure year for several reasons. It was around this time a generation born just before or during the Second World War was beginning to reach economic, political and cultural maturity. Those people knew nothing of life and attitudes before the war, and yet all the people in positions of power and authority seemed to be of pre-war generations, with values that seemed out of date. The younger generation of around 1960 in general had quite different concerns from those of its elders, and challenged traditional views perhaps more seriously than had any previous generation. Some evidence of, and reasons for, this are provided in Chapter 1.

This, to some degree, led into what became known as the age of permissiveness in the 1960s, in which the moral values of older gener-ations were discarded. A symbol of that rupture with the past occurred late in 1960 when Penguin Books were prosecuted for publishing the uncensored version of D. H. Lawrence's novel *Lady Chatterley's Lover*, which for over thirty years, since it had been written, had never appeared in full in Britain. When the 1959 Obscene Publications Act was brought to bear on it the trial jury declared the book not obscene. The verdict was considered either the end of civilisation, or the beginning of it, depending on the commentator's definition of being civilised. That was perhaps more a question of generation differences than purely political ones. Bright young intellectuals of the right, as well as of the left, were triumphant. Norman St John-Stevas, who later became a Conservative minister, for example, wrote in the *Daily Telegraph*, a very conservative newspaper, an article strongly in favour of greater liberalisation. The trial verdict certainly heralded, and contributed to, the beginning of new attitudes to sexual behaviour and language.

In the area of economics it was from about 1960 that government strategy changed. This change was not a simple development of earlier policies, but marked the introduction of different values into economic thinking. It occurred in conflict, as the historian Keith Middlemas has recorded: 'prolonged and often acrimonious debate in Cabinet from January to July 1961 shows the bleaker side which had already appeared in 1960'.[2] The economic world was dramatically different from that of the end-of-war period: 'What had once been seen as a political contract written in very general but enabling terms, was judged, seventeen years later, to be an inadequate rulebook for what had become the principal contemporary requirements: adjustment to change and economic growth.'[3] As a response to those 'principal contemporary requirements' the government, and subsequent governments, became more interventionist, attempting to control, or influence, national economic performance more directly.

The 1950s were virtually dominated by Conservative governments, but the first general election of the sixties saw a shift to Labour. Apart from the period 1970–4 the Labour Party was in office from 1964 to 1979, and that can be seen as part of the wider social transformation dating from just after 1960.

The transformation from Britain being an imperial power was also completed around that time. The change of name from Empire to Commonwealth had already occurred, and the shift in attitudes followed. The historian Kenneth Morgan has commented, 'The Commonwealth remained in large measure a ceremonial affair after 1960.'[4] It is significant that Britain first made application to join the European Common Market in the following year. Britain's world role appears to have changed to some extent from about 1960.

All the transformations of attitudes, values, beliefs involved in these features of British life are centred around 1960. None were entirely straightforward, and aspects of the complexities will be explored in more detail in the body of this book.

4   *Introduction*

Sequence of Events

I have included an outline Selected Chronology partly because when I
started writing this book I looked for an easily accessible list of basic facts,
and could not find one – so all the details had to be pieced together from
memory and a lot of different sources. That was time consuming, and I
hope this brief Chronology will be helpful in saving your valuable time.
However, no such list can contain everything of relevance, but within the
selection of events I have tried to provide as practical a framework as
possible in the space.

The inclusion of the Chronology does not mean I think you should
spend hours trying to memorise it. The old-fashioned way of studying
history seemed to be mostly a matter of learning dates, but the subject is a
very great deal more interesting and exciting than that. Dates are not
important just in themselves, simply to be memorised – or mesmerised, as
a friend of mine would punningly express it – but being aware of them, or
having easy access to the information, is important. History is a factual
subject, and it is also an interpretive one because those facts need to be
interpreted, in political and/or sociological (and perhaps other) ways.
Knowledge of history enables you to know what happened: understanding allows you to see why and how it occurred, and to appreciate the
political, social, and sometimes cultural, consequences. For example, it is
an undeniable fact that the Conservative Party gained a majority of seats
in Parliament in the 1983 general election, but – as you will see in Chapter
2 – interpretations of how that fact occurred, and the consequences
stemming from it, differ. History and politics are there to be analysed, for
the details to be taken apart, and analysis of that fact is diverse. Also some
of the aspects of society we take for granted are the results of it.

Another factor in this kind of study is the importance sometimes of
knowing the broad sequence of events in order to understand them. The
relationship of the facts in time can be vital to a real comprehension, and
therefore, interpretation, of them. As another example, to take a rather
extreme illustration, someone who thought the government's change of
basic economic policy in the mid-1970s occurred before inflation and
unemployment began to rise critically might form the impression that the
new policy created the crisis. The sequence of events, however, was that
inflation and unemployment had begun to rise and it was only after this
had become evident that the government changed its policy. We might
then argue that the government adopted new tactics in order to attempt to
cure the problem. A different interpretative difficulty occurs in the 1980s,

when the government did not change its policy even though the un-employment rate was rising. Interpretations of that are matters of politics as well as of history. That is one of the features that makes the whole area of social studies so much a subject of argument, not a simple matter of learning dry facts.

The Chronology is described as Selected because many events have been left out. That is inevitable, because space is limited. If you look at a publication such as *Keesing's Contemporary Archives* you will see that several hundreds of thousands of words are used for *each* year's events. The writers of all history, politics and social studies books select the events they analyse, and select the sources they present, from an enormous range of available information and documents. The Chronology here is Selected on the same basis as the material in the body of the book is selected. I think those items are more important than the ones omitted. Another writer might well choose entirely different events and evidence in the same period. We all have personal preferences, and you must always test anyone's views against someone else's.

The Selected Chronology is also described as outline because it does not provide precise dates, grouping events only into years. Although it is necessary to have some idea of the sequence of events, it is not always a requirement to know exact days and months. Where they are important, in the case of general elections for example, you will generally find them indicated in the body of the book.

Sometimes precise dates can even be a little misleading. Historians usually refer, for instance, to Acts of Parliament in terms of a year, rather than a more accurate date: the 1968 Race Relations Act, the 1975 Sex Discrimination Act, and so on. Each Act came into operation on a specific date, but it became an Act on another date when receiving the Royal Assent, and on an earlier date it was accepted by the House of Lords, and previous to that was the date of approval by the House of Commons. An Act first appears in Parliament as a Bill, and the day of the First Reading precedes months of debate. Any of these dates might be the relevant one for any Act of Parliament, but perhaps more important is the fact that most Acts are discussed and argued over for months previous to all that process. The atmosphere of discussion in society as a whole, during that period, is crucial. The *processes* are at least as vital as the final fact. Therefore treat the outline as a guide to sequence, not a rigidly confining mental prison.

Perception and Prejudice

History, politics and social studies involve relative judgements. It may be
difficult for anyone who has grown up in an age in which more than two
million people are registered as unemployed, and where that is taken to be
entirely normal, to comprehend how governments, and society in general,
worried in the early 1970s about unemployment reaching up towards a
figure of one million. Yet, as David Dutton has recorded, Edward Heath,
the Conservative prime minister 'was particularly shaken when unemployment reached one million early in 1972'.[5]

   We cannot understand history or politics fully if we do not see them, at
least partly, from the point of view of the time and society being studied.
For that reason, in this book I have quoted quite a number of popular
contemporary sources. Historical analysis has the advantage of hindsight,
being able to look at past events from the perspective of what happened
after them. People at the time guessed at what events might lead to, but
obviously did not know for certain. Their responses to crises, for instance,
do not always appear now to have been the most sensible ones – but that is
because today's past was their future. They could only speculate, and were
often wrong. We are following the same processes today, and no doubt
history will pass some harsh judgements on our intelligence too. Atmosphere is as important an element of history and social attitudes and
behaviour as fact, and I hope the references to newspapers, journals,
pamphlets and politicians' actual words will help you understand
something of the feelings of the people making decisions, whether as
cabinet ministers or humble voters.

   Because I do not want to express an idea of political and social history
as a story, a mere narrative of events tumbling after one another without
any particular reason, I have organised the chapters of this book around
themes. However, that in itself leads to an artificial reading of them. My
discussion of economics and general elections in Chapter 2, for instance,
can give a false impression of British politics if taken out of the wider
context of the book. I think economic issues were usually the most
important ones, and try to provide documentary evidence to support that
view, but other issues came into the debates too. In the 1970s trade union
activity, for example, was a recurring factor, though that is not looked at
until Chapter 3. You must always be aware that social studies in general
involves holding together many threads. That is part of its pleasure, it is
like weaving a mental carpet – or, to change the simile, putting together a
complex intellectual jigsaw.

I think it is important, as well as more interesting, not to see history – whether specifically of politics, economics, society, or any combination of those disciplines – as a simple continuous straight line, one fact leading directly to the next without any complications. There is more than one way of interpreting an event when it happens. We know that from the debates of today, and I hope the quotations from newspapers and politicians help to illustrate it in regard to recent history. Also, analysts and commentators are human beings and have their own opinions, which leads them sometimes to differ from one another in their interpretations. I have tried to bring that out too, occasionally, by quoting examples.

The activities with which this book is concerned entail conflict: decisions are made in the course of conflict, or in attempts to avoid it; and then interpretation can be contentious. Tension runs through history. The tensions between different groups and interests within society provide the dynamic that creates the struggle for change. Conflicts between classes, generations, ideologies, beliefs etc. may all set up a contest for power. Often the tension is clear; in politics, for instance, it can frequently be categorised broadly as between left and right-wing views.

Sometimes, however, there is ambiguity, unclarity, when the lines do not run straight as might be expected. There can even be apparent contradiction, paradox, when the unexpected happens. In the 1960s, for example, racism brought together two sections apparently with nothing in common. Elements of the extreme high-Tory right and of the proletariat with a strong reputation for strike action against capitalist employers joined forces in wanting limits to coloured immigration, and even called for enforced repatriation of black and brown members of the working classes. Another illustration can be taken from the 1990s, when the far right of Conservative and the far left of Labour MPs, despite being metaphorically at one another's throats most of the time, combined in their opposition to the European Community's Maastricht Treaty. The paradoxes of politics and history are always there to break ideas that want the subject to proceed in regular, uncomplicated straight lines.

History, politics, social studies, British Studies, are for enjoyment, whether as a subject for serious academic study, or as something to read about in idle hours: always a challenge, full of surprises. This book is my attempt to express some useful and interesting information and ideas about a fascinating subject, whether you have lived through it or have just come to it.

Chapter 1 Idealism and Reality: the 1918–60 Background

1. Britain between the World Wars

The Great War of 1914–18 ended with the defeat of the main external enemy, Germany. Amidst the general feeling of relief, there was also a belief amongst different classes and sections of British society that a new Britain should be built. This agreement amongst people and groups who disagreed about other matters is usually called by historians a consensus. In this case the consensus, or general agreement, was that the internal enemies in pre-war British society – such factors as class discrimination and privilege, poverty, unemployment, slums, epidemic disease – should also be defeated. It was widely thought that the fundamentally divided, class-ridden and socially unjust society that had existed up until 1914 was no longer acceptable or relevant. The nation had come together in a wartime consensus, and many people believed that unity must be sustained, partly for the benefit of the country as a whole as it faced the post-war world, and in part as a reward to the deprived sections of society who had made great sacrifices in order to contribute to and support the military effort.

It is significant that the general election held in December 1918, a month after the end of the war, was the first in Britain in which women were allowed to vote. The change in the law was widely seen as a reward to women for their support of the war effort; for example, their labour in the munitions and armaments industries, and the general way in which many jobs previously performed by males had been satisfactorily undertaken by females during the absence of the men in the armed services. Women were still denied complete equality with men at the voting booths, but most females over the age of twenty-nine – twenty-one for men – were enfranchised, that is, allowed to vote, and in a 1919 by-election – an election that takes place for parliament between general elections – the first woman Member of Parliament was elected.

Another aspect of the government's mentality of repaying, or recompensing, its citizens can be seen in its promises to provide a 'fit country for heroes to live in' and 'homes fit for heroes'. These slogans were identified with the wartime prime minister David Lloyd George, and evidently suited the mood of the time, for the radical historians Cole and Postgate have recorded that in the general election of December 1918 his 'coalition ... secured a tremendous victory'.[1] Social and economic policies that would ensure material well-being for everyone, equality and social justice, were promised for a glorious future. In both the slogans quoted above, the word 'heroes' projects the common soldier in particular, but by implication the masses as a whole, in an heroic role: the victors of war who have earned the right to be treated better than they were in the past.

Despite those hopes, injustice, poverty, inequality and the consequent discontent quickly reappeared. The process of disintegration emerged dramatically in the General Strike of 1926 – the only occasion on which such an action has been taken in Britain. Three years later worldwide economic depression eventually precipitated, or caused, a profound British political crisis, and any remaining hopes of consensus had to be abandoned. The historian Charles Mowatt has observed: 'the effort was made to find a better society by returning to the prewar order purged of its grosser inequalities. By 1931 it was clear that the effort had failed.'[2] There were many contributory factors, some of them outside the control of the British government, and it is possible to argue that the initial impetus for reform came from political opportunism rather than idealism. History is open to interpretation, and Lloyd George's original motives, and the nature of the reality that prevented his aims being achieved, are open to analysis in different ways.

2.   The Impact of the 1939–45 War

The situation of 1918–19 was to some extent replicated, or repeated, in 1945. It was during the Second World War (1939–45) that the Great War became known as the First World War. The earlier conflict had been fought as 'the war to end all wars', and was therefore conceived as the last, and only, world conflagration rather than the first – with the implication that it would inevitably be followed by at least one other. During the Second World War there was a strong sense that the First World War had not solved fundamental political and social problems, and a feeling that the opportunity missed after 1918 should not again be allowed to escape.

This may be illustrated by two facts. The wartime coalition government commissioned an inquiry into ways in which aspects of social inequalities and economic deprivation could be overcome after hostilities had ceased and the war had been won. The Beveridge Report of 1942, written in the depth of the war, took an extremely radical stance on reconstruction: 'Now, when the war is abolishing landmarks of every kind, is the opportunity for using experience in a clear field. A revolutionary moment in the world's history is a time for revolutions, not for patching ... an attack upon Want ... Disease, Ignorance, Squalor and Idleness.'[3] In 1944 the wartime government accepted most of the Report's recommendations. Again the motivation may have been a mixture of genuine idealism and of opportunism, a need to give people making terrible sacrifices a source of hope for the future.

In 1944, the penultimate year of the war, the Butler Education Act was also seen, or perceived, to create new opportunities for large groups of the populace who had previously been deprived of anything more than a very basic education. In the House of Commons R. A. Butler spoke specifically of providing a 'synthesis ... between manual and intellectual skill and between those better and less well endowed' (*Hansard*, 19 January 1944). It can be argued that these words reveal an unconscious belief that 'intellectual skill' is 'better' than 'manual', and that even in the act of attempting to create equality of educational opportunity Butler confirms traditional, conservative values. In this case the anti-Butler argument is that he had no real interest in synthesising, bringing together as one whole, 'those better and less well endowed' pupils, and that by using the expression 'less well endowed' he built in, or enshrined, a belief in natural inequality in the Act itself. This may be true, but there was also a genuine mood of idealism behind the framing of the Bill, and its acceptance by Parliament. Butler, in introducing the Education Bill, referred specifically to the future beyond the war effort:

> Let us hope that our work together ... will carry into the years of victory the thirst for service and advancement, as well as the common sharing of experience and opportunity which we have at present. .... Plato said: 'The principle which our laws have in view is to make the citizens as happy and harmonious as possible.' Such is the modest aim of this Bill.   (ibid.)

A phrase such as 'the common sharing of experience and opportunity' emphasises the broad agreement, the consensual unity, that is perceived in society. Even so, there were a few rigidly conservative Members of Parliament. The quotation from the classical works of the ancient philosopher Plato may have been an attempt to make a fundamental reform more easily acceptable to them. On the other hand, it may be interpreted more cynically as affirming Butler's view of true education, familiarity with the classics. This view of Butler's speech would see his ideas on education having little contact with the needs of most common people, to whom ancient philosophy was thought to have no relevance.

Whatever the motivation for the Education Act, the words of Butler did express a general, prevalent, mood for change. There was a desire in the country not simply to return to pre-war conditions; this can be seen, was manifested, in the result of the 1945 general election. For the first time the Labour Party was given an absolute majority over all other parties in Parliament. Pauline Gregg's analysis is fairly typical among historians: 'It was clear that the workers, and a considerable section of the middle classes, were distrustful of Tory social policy.'[4] The result was taken as a mandate for profound changes, and in its initial period in power, 1945–50, the Labour Government created, for instance, a thorough national health service; fundamentally revised and improved financial benefit services to those in need; nationalised a number of basic industries, such as the production of coal, iron and steel, and the essential services provided by the Bank of England, railways, civil aviation and other transport areas; and brought into public ownership the utilities of gas and electricity. Over 20 per cent of the nation's economy was taken into central control.

The idealism inherent in the government's social and economic pol-icies, the desire to create justice and equality, to banish poverty and deprivation, and the belief that it was possible to achieve those aims in practical terms, came to grief against several realities. Both at the time, and since, the nature of the achievement was, and has been, questioned. The political struggles over nationalisation were extremely bitter. There was, for example, a split on the issue of compensation for the owners of the industries that were nationalised: shareholders thought payment was not enough and unjust; some people with more socialist tendencies believed no compensation at all should be paid. Whilst Conservatives thought nationalisation was wrong, socialists wanted more of it, including taking all land into public ownership – a policy so controversial it was never even seriously considered by the Cabinet.

These controversies demonstrate, exemplify, the two main attitudes to the Labour Government of 1945–50, and also to the one that followed it from 1950 to 1951 after re-election, headed by Clement Attlee: the right wing saw them as dangerously close to Soviet Communism, the left perceived them as insufficiently socialist, as too compromised with capi-talism. Those contemporary attitudes have been continued by subsequent historians, as Kevin Jefferys has noted: 'The Attlee governments have no shortage of detractors. ... Commentators on the political right have attacked the post-war government for introducing too much socialism. ... The major complaint of left-wing critics, nevertheless, has been that the Attlee years did not see enough socialism.'[5]

The situation in the late 1940s was complicated by international politics – western Europe had been devastated by the war, and was economically reliant on Marshall Aid from the USA; eastern Europe was under the influence, if not actual control, of the USSR (Union of Soviet Socialist Republics, which was dominated by Russia and organised in Moscow). The world appeared to be divided between Washington and Moscow. The British government did not necessarily want to be in either camp, although – despite old Tory fears that identified socialism of even a moderate kind with Russian Communism – it was much more inclined towards America. A purely independent or neutral position was hardly possible.

3. Conservative Power in the 1950s

In any event, at the 1950 general election the Labour Party was returned to power with such a tiny majority, of only five seats, that in the following year they were obliged to go to the country again in another election. In 1951 the Conservative Party won the election and remained in power for thirteen years. As usual, there are diverse opinions on why the Labour Party failed to maintain effective power, and eventually lost it completely. W. N. Medlicott has maintained that the government gave 'the impression of divided counsels and of technical inability to cope with the economic problem'.[6] Certainly there was in-fighting between some individual members of the government, and recurrent economic crises – although to some extent those had international causes. There was a view at the time, which has persisted, that the government was not bold enough in the socialist direction, that it alienated the idealism of some of its supporters. David Dutton has commented that 'Labour's chief electoral strategist, sought to commit the party to a policy based on consolidation rather than innovation in order to retain the middle-class vote which Labour had been so successful in winning in 1945'.[7] Although it was not a success in 1950 the strategy was pushed even further during the 1951 election campaign: 'The party's manifesto was even more moderate. ... It did not even contain the word socialism.'[8]

There was also a psychological element at work during those campaigns. Six years of sacrifice under war conditions had been followed by a further period of hardship, of general austerity, which appeared to have no definite end. Some goods were still actually rationed, and many others in short supply. The political idealism that argued collective welfare was worth individual sacrifice could triumph in the immediate aftermath of war, but five and six years later that ideal was encountering the reality of personal material aspiration. Jefferys offers a summary of this interpretation: 'austerity was the primary cause of voters' disaffection'.[9]

History, and politics, though, are full of apparent contradictions, paradoxes. The transformation of the Labour Party's enormous parliamentary majority of 146 seats in 1945 into a Conservative Party victory of 17 MPs in 1951 was not in fact a clear decision by the electorate. Writing of the 1951 election, that saw the beginning of thirteen years of Conservative rule, Arthur Marwick has rightly warned against 'not readily generalizing about the country, or the electorate, voting this way or that way, or choosing this or that ... actually more people voted Labour in this election than voted Conservative, and more people voted Labour than had voted Labour in 1945'.[10] Labour lost votes in the crucial constituencies in which middling-class voters held the balance of power, and therefore, because of the nature of the electoral system, lost a disproportionate number of seats in Parliament. It might be thought of as a revolt of those who were growing relatively affluent, and had no particular political class allegiance.

Certainly the 1950s was a decade characterised, at least in part, by general increasing material affluence. The degree to which that was due to the specific policies of the Conservative governments, which held power between 1951 and 1964, or to a global recovery from the aftereffects of world war, depends on political perspective. Whatever the cause, the fact that for a great many people individual disposable income grew is undeniable. It was in the 1950s, for example, that television sets became thought of as almost a necessity, car ownership expanded considerably and the mass charter foreign holiday was born, to itemise only three aspects of ordinary life that are now considered normal, but in 1950 would have seemed to many people highly unlikely.

4. The New Age of the 1950s

The change, transition, from austerity to affluence, from an emphasis on collective welfare to individual materialism, through the decade of the fifties, may perhaps be seen as symbolised by the accession of a new monarch in 1952, and her coronation as Elizabeth II in the following year. The idea of a new epoch, a fresh start in national life, was strong. The historians Alan Sked and Chris Cook, looking back, wrote: 'people looked forward to a second Elizabethan age ... to enhance their hopes of national recovery and glory'.[11] At the time, the *Daily Herald*, amongst other newspapers, welcomed the coronation as the dawn of 'the New Elizabethan Age' (Leader, 2 June 1953).

The idea, or concept, of a new Elizabethan age certainly caught the imagination of the country, with its popular connotations – no matter how inaccurate in fact – of the reign of Elizabeth I having been a Golden Age typified by romantic buccaneering pirates and powerful individualist explorers and colonists. It was not a period of culture and Shakespeare that was projected, but one of Drake and Raleigh, of Britain ruling the high seas and the new worlds. In Plymouth, for example, a seaport popularly associated with the defeat of the Spanish invasion force of 1588, there was a model of Queen Elizabeth I and Sir Francis Drake witnessing the representation of a famous naval victory. If Britain had lost much of its international power since 1945 there was a hope it could be regained in the new Elizabethan age.

On a more mundane, practical level the coronation of Elizabeth II gave enormous impetus to the sale of television sets. It is not a pure coincidence that a law enabling commercial television to be set up in competition with the BBC was passed in 1954, the year following the boom in sales of receivers. In 1955 commercial television companies began broadcasting their own programmes. This development enshrined the notion of viewers' choice of channels, of individuals being free to make their own decisions about their own leisure time, rather than being restricted to what might seem to be an almost totalitarian, monolithic central control.

5. Rebellion in the 1950s

Whilst in some ways the decade was one of increasing prosperity, and perhaps, complacency, in other ways it was one of the birth of the spirit of rebellion, of embryonic revolt, that eventually gave rise to later more powerful and violent demonstrations. By the mid-fifties a generation was emerging who had not experienced as adults the privations of wartime, the acceptance of authority and the belief that it was necessary and ultimately – if not in all particular cases – effective. The newer generation did not necessarily accept the wisdom of age, and because of increasing prosperity had more disposable income than their parents had enjoyed. It was through, and with, that relative prosperity they expressed their independence.

That revolt can be seen in diverse areas of social activity. It partly forms the tension with increasing materialism, and the self-satisfaction that material well-being brought to many people, which runs through the decade.

6. Rebellion in the Streets and Cinemas

A sign of popular rebellion on the streets was the appearance of the phenomenon commonly known as 'teddy boys'. The name came from a colourful and comparatively extravagant form of dress very loosely re-lated to the Edwardian period of almost fifty years earlier. It was an easily identifiable alternative uniform that could be seen as a statement against social uniformity, a refusal to accept the rules and conventions of a society formed by older generations – those with political power – during the war years. It could be seen too as a rejection of austerity, an assertion of youth's new economic strength, and a determination to spend rather than save. Although there was no necessary correlation, or link, between teddy boy dress – female youth had its own extravagant fashion, but the male image was the one generally projected – and violence, they became synonymous in popular perception, which identified the style of dress with violent, anti-social behaviour.

This can be seen in the events of 1956 when the Bill Haley film *Rock Around the Clock* began to be shown in British cinemas. However tame and innocuous it looks now, at the time it roused great passions, and became an aspect of youth's assertive rebellion against many traditional values and codes of behaviour. At the time, newspapers reported with shock that the film caused riots in cinemas. Even *The Times*, a deliberately un-sensational publication at that time, reported incidents in which 100 or more young people were forcibly removed from cinemas, and then fought with police (for instance, the edition of 4 September 1956). A police constable giving evidence in court described the crowd as 'ranting and raving', suggesting a kind of group madness, which was certainly out of keeping with the discipline and control of a slightly earlier period.

The *Daily Herald*, in the journalistic traditions of a more popular newspaper, went for a broader approach, bringing together its reports on various disturbances:

> The rockn'roll kids go crazy
>
> Rhythm-crazed Teddy boys and their girls struggled with police in 'rock 'n' roll' riots ... several arrests were made after wild jitterbugging scenes during the showing of the jazz film 'Rock Around the Clock' ... youngsters worked themselves into a wild frenzy.... Girls spat in policemen's faces as they marched off youths in Edwardian clothes.
>
> (3 September 1956)

Although this paper uses the more slangy, or colloquial, style in referring to the music, it still presents it in inverted commas, not quite sure that it is acceptable English. In this report the term is actually spelt in two ways, revealing the uncertainty within the newspaper itself between the sub-editor who provided the headline and the reporter who wrote the main story. The disagreement is caused by the newness of the words, and of the concept itself.

The report implies that it condemns the behaviour by its repeated use of such words as 'crazy', 'crazed', 'wild', 'wild frenzy', all again suggesting some kind of mass madness. There is also, of course, the image of girls spitting in policemen's faces – which would have been especially unpleasant to most readers. The newspaper directly correlates, or links, the music, violence and 'Teddy boys ... in Edwardian clothes'. The word 'jitterbugging' was associated mainly with the USA and perhaps suggests an alien influence. Certainly the film was made in the US, although linking rock 'n' roll with 'jazz' shows that the writer, and maybe the readers, were not musically sophisticated, as the two kinds of music were entirely different. Perception, ways of seeing, and prejudice are more important in these areas than actuality or real facts.

7. Suez and the Mass Demonstration

If the cinema riots were social and working-class, it is interesting that in the same year, 1956, there were also mass political – and mainly middling-class – demonstrations against the government. They were of a completely different calibre or type from those of the Teddy boys (and girls), but they too represented a rejection of traditional received wisdom, the idea of the elders of the state, and its constitutionally appointed guardians, being infallible.

Britain and France had exercised control over the Suez Canal since the nineteenth century, and when it was nationalised by Egypt in 1956 both Britain and France invaded the area when negotiations appeared to have failed. Some people agreed that it was a reasonable and necessary political response, but others saw it as a return to brash imperialist militarism. The military campaign lasted only a few days but the outcry was immediate and not afraid to engage in violent confrontation with the police if necessary. The government was shocked, and ultimately the prime minister, Sir Anthony Eden, resigned, to be replaced by Harold Macmillan. This was certainly not simply the result of public outrage, and the USA's condemnation was probably the crucial influence throughout the episode, but the protesters did have some influence and, to some extent, it was considered a victory for a new style of active public participation in political decisions, as against the old form, of ordinary people merely accepting the policies and attitudes handed down to them from above.

Although there was no direct link between the Suez demonstrations and the Campaign for Nuclear Disarmament, CND was formed only just over a year after that new-found political activity of civil disobedience erupted. It had a programme of change, and an articulate membership, as Kenneth Morgan has commented of its formation and first Easter march: 'It was most notable for its wide range of middle-class activists. Many of them found ... CND an appropriate vehicle for wider cultural discontent with the supposed materialism and cynicism of Macmillan's Britain. ... It drew in many more thousands inspired by a moral gesture of this kind to a degree unthinkable in conventional politics.'[12] This movement of the 1950s can in some ways be seen as the ancestor of the mass demonstrations of the following decades.

8. Immigration and Racism

Other sections of the populace with 'cultural discontent' expressed it in a less 'moral' form. The rebellious challenge to the authority of law could also be very ugly. In 1958 there was serious black/white racial conflict in the Notting Hill area of London, where a concentration of West Indian immigrants had settled during the previous ten years. There was a considerable number of immigrants from the Caribbean in Nottingham, too, where race riots also occurred. Yet other areas that had attracted immigration, such as Yorkshire and the West Midlands, remained calm.

It was a new phenomenon in, or feature of, British social life, and John Solomos has in retrospect provided one interesting perspective on it: 'The 1958 race riots ... are commonly seen as an important watershed in the development of racialised politics in Britain. It is certainly true that the events ... helped to bring to national prominence issues which had previously been discussed either locally or within government departments. The riots themselves consisted of attacks by whites on blacks but this did not prevent them being used as examples of the dangers of unrestricted immigration.'[13] There may have been many reasons for the racial outbreaks occurring in 1958 in London and Nottingham, but regardless of the specific causes at that particular time and in those places, the issues both of racial relationships and of government attitudes, largely conveyed through laws, have remained central and very controversial, contentious, features of British life and politics, provoking extremely heated debate – another legacy of the fifties that became increasingly important during the following decades.

The apparent contradiction, paradox, of the 1950s, and one that has informed British history ever since, stemmed from the tension between dual forces. On one hand there was the reality of complacent materialism, people prepared to accept things as they were and just enjoy increasing material prosperity; on the other hand there was the idealism of a potential new order – which was active, participative, challenging. Of course that simple equation of one force against another is complicated because the active challenging was destructive – as in the case of racism – as well as constructive. It was in fact part of the reality of intolerance against the liberal idealism of tolerance. However, the idea of a basic duality has some validity and was shown in artistic culture too.

9. Rebellion in the Theatre

In that eventful year of 1956 the complacency of middling-class theatre, typified by a drawing-room setting, was shattered by a new dramatist. John Osborne's aptly entitled play *Look Back in Anger* inverted all the accepted theatrical conventions, and illustrates a social fracture.

Instead of representing an elegant drawing room in a fashionable area, Osborne's stage set is a 'one-room flat in a large Midland town'.[14] The main female character is of upper middling-class background, but her stage situation parodies, or satirises, the conventional opening. She is revealed 'leaning over an ironing board. Beside her is a pile of clothes' (p. 10). This was possibly the first time a play had ever begun with a woman ironing on stage, and the shock to audiences was considerable. To some it appeared to be an insult, to others it displayed invigorating, exciting genius. The character is not dressed within fashionable theatrical convention, but in a 'grubby ... skirt' (ibid.) and wearing a man's shirt. The music of the play is specifically jazz, rather than light orchestral, and the dialogue is not concerned with cocktail parties or mild middling-class anguish, but confronts issues such as social class and political power. Jimmy Porter rails against his wife's brother:

> you've never heard so many well-bred commonplaces coming from beneath the same bowler hat. The Platitude from Outer Space ... he'll end up in the Cabinet one day ... he and his pals have been plundering and fooling everybody for generations. ... His knowledge of life and ordinary human beings is so hazy, he really deserves some sort of decoration for it – a medal inscribed 'For Vaguery in the Field' ... he's a patriot and an Englishman, and he ... seek[s] sanctuary in his own stupidity.   (p. 20)

The play was performed six months before the Suez crisis, and in retrospect its attack on the intelligence of cabinet ministers, and the class structure of privilege that produced them, seemed to be vindicated, supported, by events. The punning satire of 'Vaguery in the Field' gained venom in the light of the military invasion.

Look Back in Anger was a box-office success, and was made into a very successful film. Osborne expressed the voice of the articulate and radical young, and his play can be taken as symbolising their rejection of the old authority, of the claims of mere materialism, and as showing the sense of frustration that ideals had been lost.

Nevertheless, enough people were happy to simply accept an improving standard of living. The Conservative Party won the general election of October 1959 by a large majority, 100 seats. So the 1960s commenced with the Tories comfortably in control at the beginning of their third successive term of government. One of their electoral slogans had been the prime minister's claim 'You've never had it so good!' Macmillan's government was sufficiently identified with affluence and materialism to be returned to office, yet the legacies of discontent and social opposition, born under that Conservative confidence, and expressed, perhaps a little prematurely in

Look Back in Anger, also entered the new decade. The history of Britain
since 1960 can be seen as a conflict of dualities, of dichotomy. On the one
hand there is submission to, or support of, a system dedicated to growing
relative wealth; against that there is an intensifying disenchantment and
discontent with a *status quo* apparently based on materialism and privilege
for a few.

Chapter 2 'Money Makes the World Go Around'

The title of this chapter is taken from a song in the popular film *Cabaret*.[1] Although the film is set in the Germany of the 1930s it appeared in 1972 and those particular words sum up a crucial sentiment in the Britain this book is exploring. The idea in the film, that 'life is a cabaret', seems especially appropriate to the history of British economics in the period from the 1950s. Governments have often sought popularity by increasing people's material wealth, but have been simultaneously afraid of doing so by too much, too quickly; or have tried to shelter the British individual's affluence in times of international economic storm. This has provided a cabaret setting in that collective moods have swung from happiness to sadness, laughter to tears, hope to fear.

There are many reasons why general elections are won and lost, but here I shall concentrate mainly on the importance of economic factors. It is not that the British people are necessarily interested in such aspects as the balance of payments, the international value of sterling, the volume of money supply and the gross national product in academic terms. However, they are, and have been, vitally interested in the related factors of their income, and prices. In the majority of the nine British general elections held so far during the last four decades of the twentieth century some facet of the economy, either directly or indirectly, has been a crucial issue.

1. 1959–64: Sex, Spies and Pockets

The 1960s began with the Conservative Party having, three months earlier, won its third term in power, with a majority of 100 seats. Yet in 1964 it lost that large majority, partly through an economic policy that was categorised at the time as 'stop–go'. The government alternately took measures to expand and contract, to speed up and slow down, economic activity. Although affluence continued to increase, in general the government was perceived to be, thought of by many people as, indecisive.

Indeed, the government was widely seen to be in disarray, the Conservative Party unable to agree within its own ranks. In addition to economic problems, a number of political embarrassments occurred. A selection of these were: in 1962, a savage cabinet reorganisation that left many Conservatives discontented without having the effect of actually strengthening the government; the unexpected loss of two seats at by-elections; and in the following year two scandals, centring around Philby and Profumo; and the eventual retirement of the prime minister, and his replacement by a rather pale, nondescript figure.

In July 1962 the prime minister, Harold Macmillan, replaced sixteen of his ministers in what was quickly dubbed 'The Night of the Long Knives' – an extremely unflattering reference, from Macmillan's point of view, to Hitler's destruction of the S.S. leadership in June 1934 after it had helped him to gain power. The scale of the operation was unprecedented, not equalled either before or since. Political correspondents wrote and spoke of Macmillan being ruthless with old friends, like a desperate surgeon cutting off the limbs of his cabinet's body. The political historian David Childs has recorded an immediate change in the perception of the prime minister as a result of this purging of his cabinet: 'Macmillan had been ridiculed as "Macwonder" and "Super Mac" ... if anything, these jibes had won him popularity. Now he was christened "Mac the knife". ... In his own party there was shock and anger.'[2] Reginald Bevins, a Conservative government minister, was in the centre of the controversy, and later recalled: 'I did not believe that a Conservative Prime Minister could survive such action. ... This was making enemies on a grand scale, enemies of those dismissed, enemies of their friends in Parliament, and shattering confidence in the Party at large.'[3]

The dismissal of the Chancellor of the Exchequer, Selwyn Lloyd, in particular was seen in terms of a sacrifice, suggesting that Macmillan was primarily concerned with protecting his own position of power as prime minister, and was willing to betray loyal servants if necessary. The action projected Macmillan in a very bad light, ruthless and self-interested. Writing of the time some years later Macmillan admitted that the manner of his action – though not its purpose, which was 'to bring some younger men into the administration' – was 'a serious error'.[4] It was certainly very bad public relations and people management. The main image of Macmillan to emerge from the episode was one of a tyrant butcher rather than a respected leader.

Although there were many reasons for Macmillan's wholesale reorganisation, the focusing on the shabby sacrifice of Lloyd, the Chancellor of the Exchequer, highlights the importance of the performance of the economy, which by 1962 was running into obvious difficulties. The problems were clearer to see, however, than any solutions.

The government's general problems were not solved by the prime minister's surgery. Another public image catastrophe struck in the year following the Night of the Long Knives. In 1951 two highly placed members of the establishment, Burgess and Maclean, had defected to the USSR when a spy-ring within the administration itself was discovered. It had long been suspected that other Communist sympathisers existed within the higher ranks of the civil service, and in 1963 the news that Kim Philby, a former Foreign Office expert, had suddenly decamped for Moscow seemed to confirm that spies did indeed still exist in the very corridors of power.

There was much speculation about a 'fourth man' who remained undetected at the time, and the establishment was widely mistrusted, as there appeared to be elements in it that were in league with the enemies of the state. The image of moral corruption and decay that came out of the Philby defection to Moscow was dramatically affirmed in the popular mind by the Profumo affair.

John Profumo was a minister in Macmillan's government in early 1963 when speculation and rumours began that he had a sexual relationship with a prostitute. There were two immediate aspects to the case for the media. As he was married, and to quite a well-known former actress, which added to the publicity value, there was the obvious moral dimension of adultery and hypocrisy. It also emerged, however, that the prostitute in question, Christine Keeler, had a high-ranking Russian diplomat as a client too. As Profumo was Secretary of State for War in a period of dramatic tension between the political West and the USSR bloc, an issue of national security also arose. Had Profumo mentioned defence secrets to Keeler, and had she passed them on to the Russian client?

In March 1963 Profumo made a statement in the House of Commons concerning his relationship with Christine Keeler: 'I last saw Miss Keeler in December 1961, and I have not seen her since ... There was no impropriety whatsoever in my acquaintanceship with Miss Keeler' (*Hansard*, 22 March 1963). That did not end the speculation and unofficial investigation, and just over two months later the government's credibility was again shaken when, under intense pressure, Profumo resigned from the cabinet, admitting that he had lied to the House of Commons. Most of the press were extremely critical of Profumo, and the *Guardian*, as the leading intellectual oppositional newspaper, was especially condemning (6 June 1963), although *The Times* at first concentrated on the personal aspects of the case rather than its political implications.

The public debate centred around whether the lie to Parliament, the immorality of adultery, or the possible national security danger, was the most important issue. After a few days *The Times*, realising the instability Profumo had caused the government, left its former rather sympathetic position towards him and came out strongly against the former minister, particularly on the issue of sexual morality. The wrath of the establishment against one of its own kind who had caused it difficulty was expressed on 13 June 1963 when *The Times* revealed that large numbers of readers had contacted the paper to support its stand against immorality. Profumo suddenly had very few friends, and the government was enormously embarrassed.

Those who wanted to disown Profumo without discrediting the government were in a difficult position. As a representative of those, the Conservative MP Nigel Birch criticised the establishment's newspaper in a parliamentary speech: 'I must say that I view the activities of the editor of *The Times* with some distaste' (*Hansard*, 17 June 1963). The paper, like Profumo, it was felt, had let the side down; the editor had stirred up more trouble than had been necessary. This kind of argument illustrates the disarray within the ruling group at that time.

Wilson, as leader of the Labour opposition, spoke in the House of Commons of 'a debate without precedent in the annals of this House. It arises from disclosures which have shocked the moral conscience of the nation. There is clear evidence of a sordid underworld network, the extent of which cannot yet be measured' (*Hansard*, 17 June 1963). Although the opposition always makes political capital from such events, on this occasion Wilson was probably voicing the views of the majority of people. He concentrated on the fact that Profumo 'chose deliberately to lie to this House' and whether 'a man in a position of high trust, privy to the most secret information available to a Government, through a continuing association with this squalid network, imperilled our national security' (ibid.). Wilson accused Macmillan of having ignored the original rumours of Profumo being involved in a ring of prostitution, homosexuality and drugs, and therefore himself bearing blame.

With the government and party in chaos by October 1963, Macmillan resigned on the grounds of ill health at the age of sixty-five, although he lived another twenty-five busy years in which he was involved in many public appearances and completed a great deal of writing. His successor was not even, at that time, a member of the House of Commons, although he became elected to a seat. He was the Fourteenth Earl of Home, and despite becoming Sir Alec Douglas-Home he was tainted with the image (however unfairly it may have been applied) of a feudal aristocrat, representing class privilege and out of touch with common realities. Initially even those newspapers who supported him felt obliged to tell their readers that Home was pronounced 'Hume'. This seemed to signify the gap between the public and the country's leader.

The general election was held in October 1964, and as the government was running up to the full five-year period of office, the 1964 spring Budget was the last big opportunity to make an impression, and cancel out the government's other embarrassments by putting money into voters' pockets – it is not an unusual tactic. In retrospect Kenneth Morgan has described it as 'pedestrian ... widely condemned as dull and unimaginative'.[5] The Chancellor of the Exchequer, Reginald Maudling, was hampered by a balance of payments crisis. A consequence of economic prosperity was a much larger growth in imports than exports. Many imports were cheaper than home-produced products, and British goods were too expensive to sell abroad in mass quantities. It was in honestly trying to contain this problem that Maudling produced his 'pedestrian' Budget that neither attacked the basic difficulties, nor increased the electorate's confidence.

By 1964 the Labour Party, having lost three successive elections, had moved away from its 1940s programme, as Morgan has commented: 'Labour's campaign concentrated less on questioning the reality of Tory affluence, and more on charges that it would manage it more efficiently.'[6] It was not the balance of payments problem as such that influenced voters. The crucial factor was the effect that might have on their personal lives, and a general loss of confidence in a party that seemed to lack real leadership or policies. Labour won the election, although with an overall majority of only four seats; but the Conservatives had lost nearly two million votes and 61 seats. To some extent people's pockets had voted.

2.   1964–70: Labour Leads

The new prime minister was Harold Wilson, who had become leader of the Labour Party just over twelve months earlier. Arthur Marwick later described Wilson as 'of the lower-middle-class, but Oxford-educated, [a] meritocrat'.[7] Marwick makes the point that the Labour cabinet was not entirely unlike the Conservative one in background, despite the differences between the party leaders: 'More than one third of the Labour Cabinet of 1964 were traditional upper-class figures ... Only two Ministers had graduated from universities other than Oxford,' these 'traditional ... figures' he referred to as 'patricians'.[8]

The smallness of Labour's majority in the House of Commons inevitably meant the government would not be able to stay in power for five years. It held office for about eighteen months, calling an election in the spring of 1966. As the 'meritocrat' and his 'patricians' had avoided falling into any obvious, large-scale crisis in that short time, Labour was trusted to continue in power, being elected with a substantial overall majority of 96 seats. Most historians agree that it was a low-key campaign, it had been a relatively short time since the previous general election, and the Conservatives had suffered some internal disputes. Although Douglas-Home had resigned the Conservative leadership in July 1965, to be replaced by Edward Heath, the party had not completely regained its poise. Heath saw that long-term economic creativity was vital: 'In the long run we shall not survive if for some reason, for some failure of will, we let ourselves drift slowly backwards into industrial failure and out-of-date technology.'[9] The economy was the crucial election issue, but with concentration on short-term concerns. According to National Opinion Poll surveys conducted at the time, the economy, in the specific form of the cost of living, was selected by voters as being the single most important issue in both the sixties' general elections.

In the following year, 1967, the underlying economic problems that had been ignored or covered up throughout the decade surfaced dramatically. As early in the new government's term of office as July 1966 there was an extremely serious sterling crisis, which the Wilson administration managed to ride out, but which caused policy rifts within the government. In November 1967 a further prolonged crisis led to a devaluation of the pound, of almost 15 per cent. An immediate editorial described the action as 'an open and humiliating admission that the [government's] policy has failed' (*Financial Times*, 20 November 1967).

Devaluation meant that the rate of exchange between the British pound and other currencies was cut, leading to increases in the price of imports and making exported goods comparatively cheaper abroad. As the *Financial Times* explained: 'The object of devaluation is to improve the balance of payments by making exports easier to sell and imports less attractive' (25 November 1967). As Britain imported so much the policy inevitably led to an increase in the cost of living.

The very unpopularity of the decision had caused its delay, and the longer it had been delayed the worse the situation had become. The economist Peter Sinclair later wrote: 'With hindsight, it is clear that we should have devalued earlier – probably as soon as 1961. The trend was reasonably evident as soon as that.'[10] A Professor of Politics, Andrew Gamble, confirms that the problems were fundamental, long-standing, and had mainly been avoided by both parties when in power throughout the decade: 'British governments persistently pursued a policy which held back investment and destroyed industrial confidence. By 1970 British productivity had fallen behind its main rivals and British industry was seriously under-equipped. ... If inflation could be mastered either by an incomes policy or by a slight increase in unemployment, then the obstacles in the path of faster expansion would be greatly reduced.'[11]

Inflation, or more particularly the cost of living, again emerges as a critical factor. The other side of that equation, income, is also vital. The cost of living is the relationship between income and prices. The general level of income could have been reduced by either 'an incomes policy', which means restricting the growth of incomes, by limiting wage and salary increases, and forms of unearned income such as dividends and rents; or 'a slight increase in unemployment'. That entails very drastically reducing the income of some people, rather than controlling that of the majority. Politically neither method would be popular, and the former, an incomes policy, was extremely difficult to enforce and regulate.

3. The 1970 Cabaret Swing

By the time of the June 1970 general election these factors were again, or had remained, crucial. A National Opinion Poll carried out in the autumn following that election, on the most important issues facing the new government, again discovered that the cost of living was considered the single most dominant one. Early in the election campaign, 3 June 1970, a *Daily Telegraph* editorial recognised that both unemployment and inflation had not only reached new crisis points, but were likely to become worse. *The Times* of 8 and 17 June emphasised a similar anxiety in the country at large. These were indeed issues that might directly affect voters' pockets, as a flood of price increases at the time illustrated.

An academic analysis of the election campaign observed the 'vital importance of an effective prices and incomes policy',[12] and an example of the problem emerging during the campaign was 'the dispute over doctors' pay'.[13] Heath called it a 'shopping basket election', and based his appeal on 'alarm about the cost of living'.[14] In the light of this concentration on pay and prices Butler and Pinto-Duschinsky conclude: 'one can still see the British elector as regularly swayed by attempts to time the increases in his real disposable income'.[15] With prices appearing to slide away from pay, 'real disposable income', money people have free to spend in any way they like after paying for the necessities of life, seemed to be decreasing.

With this situation occurring after six years of Labour rule it is perhaps not surprising that the Conservative Party were elected with a comfortable majority of 30 – although it is worth noting that only one third of the electorate voted Conservative. Twenty-eight per cent did not vote at all, and that may be taken to illustrate either apathy in general, or a large section of the population being disillusioned, or disenchanted, with politicians in particular, and having no faith in either party being able to improve the overall economic situation or solve any other fundamental problems.

Within a week of the ballot the *Daily Telegraph* (24 June 1970) editorial returned to the theme with which it began the campaign, seeing the government's prime task as saving the economy. It was partly in pursuit of that salvation the government formed by Edward Heath in 1970 came to grief.

4. Heath's Coal and Oil Downfall

The government had control, or influence, over a large number of pay increases. This was as the direct employer of people working in the public sector – civil servants, teachers, the armed services, and so on – or as the controlling financial decision-maker for the nationalised and publicly owned industries. At the time those included the railways, coal, gas, electricity, water, all crucial to the national economy and employing a great many workers. The argument put forward was that if the government were able to limit pay increases in these important areas it would help private industry's employers to keep a tight rein on the pay rises of their employees.

The political economist Michael Nevin has outlined the response to the situation in October 1970: 'the Heath Government laid down guidelines for the level of public sector pay settlements in the form of the "N-1" policy. The notion behind this policy was that each pay award in the public sector should be 1 per cent lower than the previous one, so that pay rises would be gradually brought down . . . set[ting] an example of wage restraint to the private sector.'[16] This was not an easy policy for the workers involved to accept, or for the government to apply, when prices continued to rise.

Just over a year later the government found itself embroiled, engaged in hostile negotiations, with the powerful NUM (National Union of Mineworkers). A strike over its wage claim was settled by an officially appointed Court of Inquiry, which fundamentally supported the miners' case; as Nevin concludes of the conflict: 'It had destroyed the "N-1" pay policy.'[17] A historian, David Dutton, has summarised it more emphatically: 'the government was humiliated by the miners' strike of 1972'.[18] Wherever you put the emphasis – whether on the economic policy in particular, or on the broader political credibility of Heath – the result was that the government had to search for other ways of managing the national economy.

They were not helped in that task by the war between Egypt and Israel just over eighteen months later in October 1973. The Yom Kippur War, as it became known, immediately affected all international relations. Basically, the Arab states of the Middle East, vital suppliers of oil across the world, placed an embargo on supplies to those nations who were not openly anti-Israeli.

By the following month the effects had become extremely critical, as a national newspaper reported: 'The oil crisis reached its blackest point last night when Esso, Britain's second largest oil group, announced that they will now start rationing' (David Hughes, *Daily Mail*, 17 November 1973). This was followed by panic buying and official reaction to it: 'Petrol hoarders were given stern warnings yesterday. It is illegal to keep petrol in a house or flat' (Paul Johnson, *Daily Mail*, 19 November 1973). Within a few days the same popular paper, which in its interests was typical of all the press, was reporting the crisis in banner headlines in the editions for 23 and 27 November 1973 (quotes by Michael Kemp and Gordon Greig, and Anthony Shrimsley, respectively):

OIL SUPPLIES AT DANGER LEVEL

ALL SET FOR RATIONING

In the midst of this the NUM again threatened to strike in support of a disputed pay claim. Just before Christmas, with the energy crisis threatening to get worse as winter became darker and colder, prime minister Heath announced emergency, some would say panic, measures. Again the *Daily Mail* was representative in its reporting. The front page on 14 December 1973 greeted its readers with the news:

> Workers to go on three-day week...
> TV to shut at 10.30
> BLACKED OUT,
> SWITCHED OFF

This decision was taken in the name of conserving energy supplies, and was naturally very unpopular indeed. Hourly-paid workers, by far the largest group of employees, were going to lose income, industrial production would fall, and everyone was about to lose the consolation of television programmes after 10.30 in the evening. People with telly-addiction were especially outraged.

The shortage of oil caused an almost immediate, huge leap in its cost, which led among other effects to a four-fold increase in the price of petrol. The quadrupling of that cost automatically led to a rise in the prices of most other products.

5. 1974: Double Cabaret Year

By early 1974 Britain appeared to be disintegrating both politically and economically. Heath called an election in February 1974. One major issue was the conflict between the government and the NUM, which was seen as a political issue (cf. Chapter 3 of this book). The other main concern was again the generally dire economic situation. This was expressed by the *Guardian*, 28 February 1974, in particular, as a concern about rapidly rising prices, rather than an interest in abstract economic theory.

In the event, the electorate seemed unsure which party would stabilise prices, and no party gained an overall majority. The Labour Party won four seats more than the Conservatives, but 37 MPs belonged to neither of those parties. Wilson returned to 10 Downing Street, but, in the circumstances, government was difficult and it was certain to be a short-lived term of office. In less than eight months Britain was again plunged into a general election campaign.

Again economic matters were clearly the main contention, in particular the relationship between price rises – usually referred to as inflation – and wage increases. Sked and Cook have observed that in 1974, 'inflation had accelerated fairly steadily... [and] Average earnings increased by no less than 25 per cent.'[19] In the circumstances it is not surprising that media coverage concentrated on those two factors. Labour was returned to power with an overall parliamentary majority of only three, but as there were 39 MPs representing a mixture of four other parties the gap between the government and the Conservatives, the main opposition party, was 42. Political manoeuvring with any of the smaller parties assured the Labour government of majorities in House of Commons votes.

6. 'Raging inflation'

In 1974 inflation was at its highest level since the Second World War, over 20 per cent. The concern about the economy shown in the newspapers before the election was continued immediately after it. In its first edition after the ballot *The Economist* stated: 'A decline has taken place in something intangible called national spirit, but that means a decline too in very tangible things. Britain's wealth and its influence have each deservedly fallen by the standards of Britain's neighbours. ... World slump, unemployment and inflation mean that the tide for a return to a freeze on incomes will come in' (12 October 1974). Here the deliberate linking of 'national spirit', 'wealth' and 'influence' indicates that economic management was seen to have far-reaching effects, much more than in the area solely of finance. In order that the problems of spirit, wealth and international influence may be solved, the article forecasts the reintroduction of a pay policy. After the demise of Heath's 'N-1', two years earlier, there had been something of a free-for-all in pay bargaining. Management, in the form of restrictions on wages and salaries, was clearly being advocated.

This was not just a matter of concern for the intellectual press. At the same time Roger Carroll in the best-selling tabloid was also urging economic action: 'A crash Budget is the first task for the Chancellor now that the crisis Election is over. ... Action to save jobs and stop companies going bust is expected. ... Even in the heat of the Election battle, all parties agreed that the price code would have to be relaxed' (*Sun*, 11 October 1974). The 'price code' was a government measure to restrain price increases, with the object of constraining inflation and holding down wage rises. It was naturally very unpopular with people running businesses, who felt that profits were being squeezed by artificially low prices. The following day the paper repeated the call for urgency: 'Nobody can argue about the new Government's top priority. *The raging inflation which threatens all our tomorrows must be halted immediately and at all costs.*' The argument behind these attitudes was that 'the price code', which restricted price rises, 'would have to be relaxed', perhaps a roundabout way, a euphemism, of saying abolished. That would mean prices increasing, but since inflation had to be '*halted ... at all costs*' – and the italics emphasise the point – the way of achieving that would be to limit, or stop, wage and salary increases.

The two publications were in some agreement, but the political consequences of their recommendations were not popular with the leaders of large trade unions. However, in 1974 inflation touched 28 per cent, and wage-rate increases averaged 26.4 per cent. In the calculation of an average, of course, many people's wage rises must be below it. Therefore the income of very many citizens, including such sections as vulnerable pensioners, who did not receive the average, were getting worse off literally by the week. Whatever anyone's political views, there was no doubting the urgency of finding a solution to the problem.

7. Economic Revolution

It proved a turning point, or watershed, in economic thinking in Britain. The political analysts Dennis Kavanagh and Peter Morris have written that there was a 'revolution in economic policy and the rejection of Keynesianism. In 1975 Denis Healey's budget abandoned the commitment to plan for full employment.'[20] The use of the concept 'revolution' indicates that the authors see it as a profound transformation in economic philosophy, not a mere slight shift of policy within the old framework of thinking. Although it could hardly have been realised in the mid-1970s, the radical changes of the 1980s stem from that 'revolution', caused by economists' and politicians' attempts to solve the problems of that time.

The debate about economic policy was between the philosophy known as Keynesianism and the concept of monetarism. I will try to explain these terms clearly in the following pages, but it is important to appreciate that the dispute was not a dry academic one between people with little impact on, or contact with, reality. Whatever anyone's political opinions, it cannot be denied that the issues of unemployment and inflation affect every person in a nation to some extent – and can completely transform for the worse the way many people live. The policies adopted, whatever they are, do have a real effect on day-to-day life.

The experience of Britain in the mid-1970s in some ways pre-figures one of the great wider European issues of the century's last decade: the transition in eastern and central Europe from Marxism to capitalism. Recent British history illustrates that capitalism takes different forms, and that the relationship between governments, people as a whole, and the practical working of capitalism is not simple and fixed. It is varied, complex and dynamic, and can be deliberately and consciously changed at any stage. Even the fairly straightfoward choice between Keynesianism and monetarism shows the diversity of methods of organising capitalism, and they are not necessarily the only possibilities available.

Until the mid-1970s the theories of John Maynard Keynes had been fundamentally accepted by both the main British political parties since 1945. There were differences of opinion about details of application, but not the basic concepts and aims. Keynes was an economist who had argued in the 1920s and 1930s that governments could intervene in the national economy to create and sustain full employment by means of fiscal policy – policies relating to public revenue. Keynesian economics has been defined as: 'concern with aggregate behaviour, especially the income generating effect of total expenditure'.[21]

Re-expressed in crude lay terms, it might be said that all governments have a fiscal policy, methods of raising public revenue, and that broadly speaking a government raises revenue through taxes, and other means, and can influence market demand by the way it spends that money. If individuals within an economic system generate income they spend it, the less income they have the smaller the demand for goods and services. Thus full employment generates high income and that maintains demand, which keeps employment high. If it works it makes both economic and social sense, since people are working, producing, consuming and happy. However, if the relation between earnings and productivity goes wrong there can be an inflationary effect, the nation begins to spend more than it is actually earning in real terms – in this case in the value of goods and services produced rather than wages and salaries paid. The government, in this instance, has to borrow money in order to sustain the system, but the borrowing is not creating any real productivity, only government debt.

Three months into the government's new term of office the Chancellor of the Exchequer, Denis Healey, made a speech that the political econ-

omist Peter Jay described, in *The Times* of 16 January 1975, as concentrating on the need to hold back inflation by restricting pay rises and money
supply. The latter would create much more unemployment in the short
term, though with the long-term objective of bringing it down again.
Healey argued that wage inflation was a primary cause of unemployment
and that public expenditure needed to be limited (this is linked to the idea
of restricting money supply). It was essentially a monetarist, as opposed to
Keynesian, policy – although those words were not used. His budgets
increased taxes and cut public spending, whilst his cabinet colleagues
achieved agreement with trade union leaders about the limitation of wage
increases.

In his memoirs Healey recalled the background to his decision, one that
changed the nature of British economic management profoundly: 'In
1974 the Treasury was the slave of the greatest of all academic scribblers,
Maynard Keynes. ... Though he died in 1946, his influence was still
dominant ... I abandoned Keynesianism in 1975.'[22] Using terms such as
'slave' and 'academic scribblers' puts forcefully an attitude about Keynes
that was almost shocking at the time, especially to left-wing thinkers.
Explaining why Keynes's influence had been so bad Healey wrote: 'his
theories had two important weaknesses when applied in postwar Britain.
They ignored the economic impact of social institutions, particularly the
trade unions .... And they ignored the outside world.'[23] Healey described
himself after that change as 'an eclectic pragmatist'.[24] In other words, he
was prepared to take any idea that appeared to be practical, from any
source – he bacame a collector of what seemed to be practical ideas.

The following year the leader of the Parliamentary Labour Party,
James Callaghan, put the new philosophy forcibly to the party's annual
conference, starting by rejecting the old (Keynesian) economic concepts:
'We used to think that you could spend your way out of a recession, and
increase employment by cutting taxes and boosting Government spending ... that option no longer exists, and that in so far as it ever did exist, it
only worked on each occasion since the war by injecting a bigger dose of
inflation into the economy, followed by a higher level of unemployment.'[25] It was a rejection, or repudiation, of the party's approach to
economics over the previous half a century. It was also an open, overt,
acknowledgement that the policies had been drastically changed.

Callaghan went on to explain that high employment would best be
achieved by 'a strong manufacturing sector of industry'. That would be
attained by the government overcoming inflation, and the 'willingness of
industry to invest in new plant and machinery'. The idea of Labour and

free-enterprise industry in cooperation was contentious, liable to create fierce debate, when considered in the light of the party's traditional attitudes to capitalism. Callaghan, as Party leader, presented the case uncompromisingly. He stated that it was necessary: 'industry is left with sufficient funds and has sufficient confidence to make the new investments.... I mean they must be able to earn a surplus ... to make a profit. ... Whether you call it a surplus or a profit, it is necessary for a healthy industrial system.... These are elementary facts of life.'[26] The fact that an assertion of capitalism's right to make a profit could be made at a Labour Party conference would have astounded people only a few years before. Concepts such as 'investment' and 'profit' had changed from being dirty words to being 'elementary facts of life', indisputable notions. The profound transformation of thinking was caused by the awful depth, and extremely critical nature, of the economic crisis. It seemed too big for the old solutions to work anymore.

The transformation, however, did not occur without bitter opposition, and it is significant that there were shifts in power within both major parties. Wilson had retired as prime minister, and been replaced by Callaghan. In the same period, the Conservative Party was also undergoing radical change. Heath was succeeded as Conservative leader by Margaret Thatcher in 1975, and that too opened the path to new economic thinking.

In the year of Callaghan's rebuttal of Keynesian economics, 1976, a leading Conservative, Sir Keith Joseph, gave the Stockton Lecture in which he stated:

> We have driven out some wealth-creators; discouraged others; shrivelled the impulse to expand and throttled enterprise. ... It is here in Britain that pseudo-Keynesian policies of demand management and deficit financing coupled with socialist attitudes to wealth creation have since the War been put most sustainedly into action. The result ... we have nearly always been at the top of the inflation and the bottom of the growth league. ... We have been surpassed by the performance of all other industrial countries.[27]

Although Joseph referred to 'pseudo-Keynesian policies', suggesting that the original Keynes's doctrines had been misinterpreted, his speech was a clear signal that all economic thinking 'since the War' – the thirty years from 1945 – was being rejected. It had caused inflation and stunted the growth of productivity. Key linked concepts in this speech that, perhaps paradoxically on the surface, connect it with Callaghan's statement to the Labour Party conference are 'wealth-creators' and 'wealth creation'. Callaghan spoke of the need for business 'confidence' and the ability of industry 'to earn a surplus ... make a profit', for it is through the investment of profit that growth expands and employment is secured or created. The theory is based on the assumption, of course, that profit would be reinvested, which by no means always happens – but certainly losses cannot lead to investment.

It was a time of intense re-thinking, and also, in 1976, the Conservative Central Office produced a booklet, punningly entitled *The Right Approach*, advancing similar arguments: 'Britain faces this new world in a weaker and relatively poor state than most of our competitors. We have suffered from low productivity and low profits, and therefore low investment and industrial stagnation. Most recently we have endured a wounding bout of inflation, leading to very high unemployment, and we are now heavily in debt'.[28] The connection between cause and effect is made partly through the emphasis of the repeated 'low', and in part by the use of 'therefore', which suggests a logical step in the argument. The economy, in this view, is caught in a downward spiral: 'low productivity' leads to 'low profits', which automatically leads to 'low investment and industrial stagnation'. Again, it assumes that high profits will be reinvested to create good economic conditions, a feature of the theory some members of the Labour Party contested, arguing that profit was not necessarily re-invested. They, however, were not in a position of real political power.

The theory of capitalist economics that was replacing the Keynesian approach was monetarism. Instead of the government spending more money in order to create employment, as Keynes directed, under monetarism it would spend as little as possible in order to cut inflation, and that would create productivity – so the argument ran. Gamble has stated the monetarist case succinctly: 'Inflation is always and everywhere a monetary phenomenon; it can be halted if the growth of the money supply is curtailed ... governments ... must aim to balance their budgets ... they must either raise their taxes or reduce their spending.'[29] The Conservative method was uncompromisingly the latter.

The Conservative Party pamphlet went on to introduce the concept of monetarism into the debate. This became the crucial doctrine of the Thatcher governments, and beyond, through the century's final decades: 'The first essential in economic management is the conquest of inflation. ... To this end, a steady and disciplined monetary policy is vital. Monetary policy will be neither stable nor disciplined unless the State's own finances are swiftly put in order ... the Government's expenditure far outruns its revenue. ... No Government can go on borrowing one pound out of every five that it spends.'[30] It is not too far from Callaghan's position. He had confronted his Labour Party critics with the argument: 'the priority is to create more wealth ... Our social policy is concerned with the distribution of wealth ... wealth must be created before it is distributed. This is where a misunderstanding ... has arisen ... on the question of public expenditure.'[31]

Both parties were coming towards agreement on the need for industry to make profits, without undue restrictions or heavy taxation, and for public expenditure to be limited. They continued to disagree on the degree of the limitation, partly because the Conservative Party saw government spending as being necessary only on bare essentials, while Labour continued to see it as a method of redistributing wealth from the richer to the poorer people in society. It is significant, as mentioned above, that in the mid-1970s both major political parties acquired new leaders and radically new economic policies almost simultaneously.

8.   1979: 'Winter of Discontent' General Election

Behind all the talk and writing about profits, industrial expansion, un-employment and public spending, was the spectre of inflation. The government's attempt to control that led it into conflict with trade unions in the winter of 1978–9, and this was a major factor in the electoral defeat of Labour in 1979.

The features of the winter of 1978–9 were an economic policy based on restraining wage rises, a number of crippling strikes, and extremely severe weather conditions. The first factor caused strikes among key workers such as ambulance drivers, whose services became increasingly vital as the weather worsened, causing more accidents, more old people and children to need hospital treatment for serious illness. In mid-January 1979 haulage drivers went on strike, threatening the delivery of food and other crucial supplies across the country. The prime minister attempted to persuade the union against industrial action, but failed.

On 11 and 12 January 1979 much of the media reported that Healey, as Chancellor of the Exchequer, was warning that the number of strikes taking place could cause two million people to be out of work within a week. At the same time TUC leaders were recorded as blaming the government's strict pay limits for the industrial disputes. In any event the government's warning was unheeded, as Sked and Cook have observed: 'On 22 January, 1½ million public service workers began a 24-hour strike.

... Water workers, ambulance drivers, sewerage staff and dustmen were among those whose industrial action was causing widespread misery in a winter that seemed unending. Under this barrage of industrial disputes, the pay policy of the government simply collapsed'.[32] The government was contemplating, or planning, emergency action to cover essential services, but faced not only opposition from trade union leaders, but conflict within its own ranks too. The more politically left-wing cabinet members tended to support the trade unionists. At the same time strike action was spreading and the weather was becoming more severe.

The episode, which in effect brought down the government and heralded nearly two decades of Conservative power, provides a nice example of how events are open to different interpretations. The prime minister at the time, Callaghan, later wrote: 'the inflation rate for September 1978 had fallen to 7.8 per cent ... the slow fall in unemployment was continuing, while domestic production was growing ... and new private investment was improving. These tangible gains had been won by intensive effort. ... Unfortunately, future events were to show that the goodwill of the TUC was not sufficient and that our critics in some of the unions and in the Party would be satisfied with nothing less than a complete abandonment of any incomes policy. This I was not prepared to do.'[33] Callaghan clearly blames his critics for creating the circumstances, the challenge to an incomes policy, that led to the downfall of the Labour government.

Clive Jenkins, one-time president of the TUC, who was involved in the negotiations, later wrote: 'Jim Callaghan's government did not deserve to be brought down. It could have been saved, although Jim must bear responsibility.'[34] In Jenkins's view the prime minister's most serious error was his insistence on an exact figure of 5 per cent for wage rises. Both sides claim the other was intransigent, whilst one of the prime minister's critics within the government, Tony Benn, recorded in his diary that Callaghan said in a private political meeting: 'The TUC simply can't help us at the moment and we can no longer rely on them.'[35] Benn's comment on this anti-trade union attitude was, 'It was a patently false statement.'[36] He recorded his own interjection as being, 'We must recognise that there is a mass-madia attack now on the trade unions of a kind I have never seen before.'[37] The emphasis in these three accounts of the crisis varies, and should be a warning against any historian's dogmatic statements about events.

The ultimate result of the conflict, however, was that the government, which had only a slender majority in Parliament, lost a vote of confidence in the House of Commons over its handling of the 'winter of discontent',

as it had become known – after the first line of Shakespeare's play
Richard III. The prime minister felt compelled to call an immediate
general election, six months before he would have needed to otherwise.
The *Guardian* leader column of 29 March 1979 showed some sympathy for
Callaghan having to face a spring general election rather than being able
to postpone it until later in the year. As the writer observed, with prophetic
accuracy, memories of the chaos and bitterness of the winter of discontent were much too strong for Labour to have a chance of winning an
election at that time. Six months of recovery through the summer might
have made a significant difference. In the event, it was the trouble caused
by the government's attempt to impose a pay policy, which itself was a
result of economic thinking about the need to contain inflation, that was a
root cause of the election having to be called at a bad time for the Labour
Party.

Within a week of the dissolution of Parliament, the calling of a general
election, the Conservative Party leader was on the attack with promises of
tax cuts, especially on earnings and savings. Clearly the state of the
national economy would again be a central electoral issue. Later in the
campaign the two main parties' strategies were summarised by the
Guardian of 26 April 1979. The Conservatives stressed law and order, and
large and immediate cuts in taxation; whilst Labour concentrated on
health, education and prices. Obviously any election is likely to have
several concerns, but it is significant that the one both parties have in
common is economic – taxes and prices – although approached from the
different angles of personal income or expenditure.

A public opinion poll revealed that many people thought Callaghan
more capable personally than Thatcher, but that they favoured Conservative policies. The *Daily Telegraph* of 30 April 1979 considered that the
central issues concerning people related to the economy. Apart from the
law and order factor it was taxes, prices, unemployment and the unions
that would decide the election outcome. Although this book looks at the
role of trade unionism separately (in Chapter 3), it is something of an
artificial division, and it is interesting to note that the newspaper includes
trade unions specifically as an aspect of the economic issues. In fact a year
before the election the Conservative MP John Biffen had written: 'The
hallmark of a decisive victory for the Right would be a British economy
where inflation was countered by monetary and fiscal policies, and where
these policies were not vitiated by powerful trade union behaviour. ...
The Tory party, in office or in opposition, should strive to secure a
political situation where these objectives are tacitly assumed to be the

framework of national policy.'[38] This proved to be a prophetic summary of the following decade or so of 'Tory' rule.

9. First Woman Premier

The Conservative Party won the election with an overall majority of 43 seats, and Margaret Thatcher made history by becoming the first female prime minister of Britain. To some observers at the time, it seemed ironic that at the end of the decade which effectively saw the beginning of contemporary feminism in Britain (cf. Chapter 5) the honour should fall to a Conservative, since it had been the political left who had been loudest in support of the feminist movement, whilst the Conservatives had rejected most feminist claims.

A front-page article of a newspaper that had supported the Conservative campaign responded to that party's success with some caution. The *Daily Telegraph* of 5 May 1979, although cheering Thatcher's victory, was also worried about possible disunity within the party concerning the relationship of Thatcher and her predecessor, Heath – who was in fact excluded from her cabinet. The leader comment of the same edition continued the subdued tone, warning of the serious problems facing the new government despite the fact that the 'winter of discontent' conflicts appeared to have quietened down. These included Northern Ireland's continuing terrorism, inflation, and in particular schoolteachers who were very unhappy with their jobs and the state of education. Crime was also becoming an increasing problem.

Commenting on the detailed voting pattern of the electoral swing to the right, the *Guardian* leader of 5 May 1979 concluded that there was some dissatisfaction with the Labour government amongst the less fortunate voters, whilst the better-off were seduced by the promises of tax cuts that would increase their affluence. This suggests a concern with individual well-being rather than collective welfare. That is, of course, the immediate response and personal view of only one observer.

The case provides an illustration of how historians have the advantage of hindsight. Fifteen years later the cautious hope with which the new government was welcomed, as against the fear that it had been elected for the wrong, basically selfish, reasons, could both be perceived in terms of what had actually happened. Inflation had been dramatically brought down from just under 10 per cent when the Conservatives took office to less than 3 per cent by late 1994, but the number of people without jobs had almost doubled. The disaffected schoolteachers of 1979 had not been won over during four successive Conservative periods of office, and in April 1994 threatened to strike over the issues of examination league tables, class sizes, teacher redundancies and appraisal. Chapter 3 of this book illustrates that the goal of ending Ulster terrorism had not been achieved within the first fifteen years of continuous Conservative rule. Indeed, killing had continued virtually unabated – for instance, in four days in June 1994 there were nine murders and nine serious woundings in Northern Ireland – although by the end of 1994 the situation was looking much more hopeful at last. The government had no success in tackling general crime, where recorded cases in the twelve months ending in mid-June 1993 rose to a record high of 5.7 million offences. There was something of an outcry when the Home Secretary admitted that he had no idea how to prevent crime. In August 1994 Peter Cadbury, a long-time subscriber of large funds to the Conservative Party, announced that he was withdrawing his financial support, specifically because of the government's failure to deal effectively with the problem of increasing crime.

The situation was summarised in a book of interviews published in June 1994:

> We are a much more fragmented nation than we used to be, and the class divisions are still pretty deep in society. There is a growing chasm between rich and poor.... The education system, which used to be second to none, no longer is.... The most difficult profession now in our society is the teaching profession. We're not giving teachers the resources or the kind of salary that will motivate them ... over the last fifteen years we've mucked about with education to such a degree that teachers are demoralised.[39]

This criticism was the more powerful because it was not made by the predictable left-wing bigot – the style reveals that – but by as respectable a commentator as could be found, George Carey, the Archbishop of Canterbury. It is significant that Carey speaks in 1994 specifically of 'the last fifteen years', putting the beginning of the decline firmly in 1979.

Behind all these issues, recognised as central at the beginning of Conservative power in 1979 by the *Daily Telegraph*, were the government's controversial economic policies. Almost fifteen years later, in February 1994, an independent review body, the Institute for Fiscal Studies, published a report – widely publicised by the mass-media – which concluded that changes in taxation created by the Conservatives had increased financial inequality, costing the lowest earners £3 per week on average, whilst the richer had benefitted by about £30 a week. In retrospect it looks as though, in this instance, the fears of greed had more justification than the cautious hopes for social unity.

10.   Thatcherism in Practice

The month following the Conservatives' election victory the new Chancellor of the Exchequer, Sir Geoffrey Howe, made his first Budget speech – significantly, on clear monetarist lines. He actually quoted Callaghan's 1976 speech, and in condemning the existing tax system echoed Joseph (both quoted above): 'a structure of taxation that might have been designed to discourage innovation and punish success' (*Hansard*, 12 June 1979). He also reiterated a point made in *The Right Approach*, about Britain's position relative to its neighbours: 'The French people now produce half as much again as we do. The Germans produce more than twice as much' (ibid.). Howe's statement of his principles of action were carried into effect throughout the following decade: 'We need to strengthen initiatives, by allowing people to keep more of what they earn . . . reducing the role of the State . . . [and] the burden of financing the public sector' (ibid.). Few people at the time realised exactly the extent of the fundamental changes those ideas would entail. They were a crucial factor in making the world of the 1990s profoundly different from that of the early 1970s.

Howe's first Budget, in June 1979, did indeed reduce the main rate of income tax, 'allowing people to keep more of what they earn'. At the same time, however, indirect taxation was increased considerably. This is largely point-of-sale taxation, which means the prices of goods and services rise because they contain an element of tax, money that goes to the government revenue fund. Tax on petrol was increased, for example, and since that adds to the cost of transporting goods there is a double effect: individuals buying petrol pay more for it, and, when shopping, are charged more for goods delivered to shops by road.

The most dramatic increase in indirect taxation made by that first Thatcher government was the virtual doubling of Value Added Tax (VAT), from 8 to 15 per cent. That is a tax added to the price of most goods and services. The effect is to tax people with lower incomes more heavily than higher-income tax payers, since those with low incomes have to spend a higher proportion of their money on essentials. The long-term result of their economic policy led successive Conservative governments between 1979 and 1994 to reduce the highest rate of income tax from 60 to

40 per cent, the main tax band from 33 to 25 per cent, but more than double VAT from 8 to 17½ per cent, and also increase the range of goods to which it is applied – for example, in 1994 VAT became payable for the first time on domestic gas and electricity. This has clearly shifted the burden of government revenue-raising away from the financially better-off citizens, as the institute for Fiscal Studies report referred to above shows.

The single most dramatic event of the term of office was the war with Argentina, after that country's invasion of the Falkland Islands in 1982. Within the organisation of this book, that action is more relevant to Chapter 6, but there was a general election in the following year, and there has been controversy amongst historians as to whether the war or the economy, or another feature, was the deciding factor in Thatcher's first electoral defence of her premiership.

Eight days before the election, the only popular tabloid newspaper to support the Labour Party had no doubt what the deciding factors should be:

The REAL Issues

What has happened to British industry . . . is frightening. . . . For the first time, we are importing more manufactured goods than we are exporting. . . . It is a decline that can be paralleled in education, housing and health.

(Daily Mirror, 1 June 1983)

A week later the paper assured its readers: 'on the supreme issue of our day – the issue of ending the criminal unemployment in our country – Labour is the only party that offers a realistic programme' (8 June 1983). For this newspaper 'the supreme issue' is, again, the economy. The emphasis on 'our day', 'our country' is based on an appeal to collective interests, an identity of mutual welfare rather than the narrow benefits to particular individuals. The phrase 'criminal unemployment' evokes a powerful feeling against the people, the criminals in this definition, who have created it. It was, certainly, a predictable result of the monetarist economic policy that unemployment would increase.

On 8 June 1983, the day before the election, the analyst of *The Times* commented of the latest opinion polls, that most people appeared to think of the catastrophically rising unemployment as a punishment for economic sins committed in the past. It wasn't that people were not interested in unemployment as a problem, but that they accepted monetarist views about its inevitability. This is not to argue that the public at large understood, or even knew, the terms Keynesian and monetarist, but they did grasp the idea of some kind of a connection between tax cuts for people in employment and an absence of jobs for other people.

As a result of polling day the Conservatives' parliamentary majority rose from 43 seats to 154, an annihilation of the opposition. A typical leftish analysis of the reasons is Marwick's: 'There were other factors, but the "Falklands factor" was the critical one in bringing them fully into play and in neutralizing whatever effective resistance there might have been to the political triumph of Thatcherism.'[40] A group of analysts from the Department of Government, University of Essex, however, have reached a different conclusion: 'Government popularity was already accelerating as a result of macroeconomic factors before the outbreak of the Falklands crisis, in particular "personal economic expectations" proved to be of critical theoretical and empirical significance. ... The Falklands crisis merely coincided with a jump in government popularity which would have occurred anyway in the wake of Geoffrey Howe's 1982 Budget.'[41] It is a question of argument as to how far the 'macroeconomic factors' carried through to the election. The fact that inflation had fallen from over 20 per cent at its peak to 5 per cent certainly caused many people's 'personal economic expectations' to improve. The cost was unemployment for the unlucky, but as *The Times* had observed that was a price a lot of voters were willing for someone else to pay on their behalf.

Obviously history becomes more a matter of interpretation than mere fact at this stage. The Falklands War did not play a large part in the actual election campaign, but that does not necessarily mean it had no importance. The Falklands victory had occurred less than twelve months before polling day and was part of the mental and emotional atmosphere of the time. Paradoxically it was the Labour Party who brought it up as an election issue at all. Perhaps that happened because the party campaign managers felt it was a hidden, covert, consideration they should bring into the open. If that was the case it appeared to backfire.

A week before polling Healey referred in a public speech 'to Mrs Thatcher's exploitation of the Falklands factor, and said that she "gloried in slaughter"'.[42] Healey subsequently called this 'one of the greatest bloomers of the campaign ... this incautious phrase. ... I meant to say "conflict".'[43] The media immediately rallied to the prime minister's defence. The disc jockey Pete Murray – who had found fame as a rebel in the 1960s – spoke eloquently on Breakfast Time television of Thatcher's compassion for the victims of the Falklands War. The *Sun* produced an interview with the widow of a man who had been awarded the Victoria Cross for Gallantry, criticising Healey and his comment. Even the liberal-minded Sunday *Observer* queried Healey's political wisdom. In its edition of 5 June 1983 the paper reported the results of an opinion poll in which the government's handling of the Falklands War was rated its greatest success.

Interestingly, the same number of people considered the Conservatives' economic policy successful as thought it was failing. The fact that the war was considered a success for the government indicates that it was at least under the surface, covertly, in voters' minds. Yet it was brought to the surface by the Labour Party – Healey never admitted that was an error, he recanted only the manner in which he had drawn it into the election debate. Those people surveyed appeared to be about equally split on the question of the economy, so that clearly some voters were not happy with the high level of unemployment.

Immediate responses to the overwhelming Conservative victory did not concentrate on either the economy or the Falklands, but on the apparent surrender of Labour. On the day before the poll *The Times* commented that Labour was paralysed, and that as a consequence Thatcher did not need to define her policies for the future. Appearing in a pro-government newspaper this was not a compliment to the prime minister, but an observation on the inadequacy of the opposition.

That notion was expanded in an anti-Thatcher election *post mortem*: 'The truth is that Labour should have had a feast of votes. . . . Instead it was left with the crumbs. . . . The voters have shown before that they will not support a split party. And since 1979 Labour had been deeply split' (*Daily Mirror*, 11 June 1983). The verdict was that the Labour Party had thrown away an election it should have won on the grounds of the government's economic incompetence. An almost immediate consequence was that Michael Foot, who had taken over the leadership of the Labour Party on Callaghan's resignation in November 1980, was himself replaced. Three months after the disastrous 1983 general election Neil Kinnock became Labour leader, with a brief to unify and repopularise the party.

Again, analysis of the actual election result was complicated by the system of first past the post in unequal electoral districts. The Conservatives in fact polled slightly fewer votes in gaining a parliamentary majority of 143 seats in 1983, than they did in winning by 43 seats in 1979. One reason was that Labour lost over three million votes, mostly to the newly formed Alliance (see Chapter 3). These points were quickly picked up on the Sunday after the results by the *Observer* of 12 June 1983. The leader-writer was aware of a possible connection between a huge election win at a time when unemployment was at its post-war highest, and the weakness of the opposition. The paper's leader was concerned with the potential problems of the following four or five years. The majority in the House of Commons was overwhelming, and outside Parliament the Labour Party again in disarray. It was a dangerous recipe, inviting an authoritarian approach from a prime minister who lacked any restraints on her prejudices, attitudes and actions.

11.   1983–7: Dogma Unleashed

The period of office was characterised by a dogmatic concern with three issues: attacking trade unions, privatising industries owned by the nation, and restricting government spending. There were, of course, other concerns too, but those three were central.

The government won two decisive victories over trade unions. Early in 1984 it successfully banned trade union membership among staff at the Government Communications Headquarters (GCHQ), despite a vigorous campaign throughout the Labour movement. Two months later the NUM began a miners' strike, against which the government was resolute. A year later the strike collapsed having achieved none of its objectives. These defeats for trade unions were proof that a new era of industrial relations had begun. In effect, although there were other factors too, very widespread unemployment had done much to sap union power.

One of the central economic features of the period was the government's policy of privatisation. This entailed changing the status of large publicly controlled and nationalised industries to private ownership. In practice this meant selling shares in such companies to the public at large, and to financial institutions. Control passed from the government, or its appointees, to a board of directors, who were in theory accountable to private shareholders. This removed the industries from the public sector.

The first large-scale operation was the privatisation of the telephone system, previously part of the General Post Office organisation, in 1984. Despite opposition from the Labour Party and trade unions the sale of shares was immensely successful, raising nearly £4 billion. Success was guaranteed because the shares were put on sale at a deliberately cheap price, and people who bought them had the opportunity to sell-on immediately at a very large profit. That was a pattern which continued throughout the period of the 1983–7 Conservative administration, and its successor. British Gas was also a very large privatisation, with the Trustees Savings Bank, British Aerospace, Britoil, Rolls-Royce, British Airports, the public utilities providing electricity and water all passing from the public to the private sector of the economy. The greed factor was clearly important in the policy's popularity. Writing of the history of the two largest operations Edgar Wilson has observed: 'of 2.3 million people who bought shares in British Telecom only 1.3 million still had them in 1989. In 1986, 4.4 million people bought shares in British Gas, but only 2.7 million retained them in 1989.'[44] This indicates that for a great many ordinary people privatisation shares were not investments, but represented a quick gain, a mere gamble, but one on which it seemed impossible to lose.

When, in May 1987, Thatcher decided to call a general election a year earlier than she needed it was partly against this background. Also unemployment had peaked at the record official level of about three and a quarter million people (13.5 per cent of the nominally working population) in 1985, and was slowly beginning to fall. In March 1987 the Budget contained a small reduction in income tax, and Thatcher had a widely publicised successful visit to the USSR.

Even before the election date was announced Labour was gearing up for action, an indication that the dissolution of Parliament a year early was not entirely a surprise. Kinnock was attempting to relaunch the Labour Party as one of potential government. The *Observer* of 29 March 1987, six weeks before the eventual polling day, reported that Labour would be concentrating on the issues of pensions, jobs, education, crime, and the National Health Service. All of these issues are directly or indirectly related to a government's economic policy.

12. 1987: Fear over Hope

During the election campaign the Conservative-supporting press affirmed that, despite high unemployment, the economy was doing well. A typical assertion ran: 'prosperity in Britain is bursting out all over. The tally for new orders being run up by our factories is now at its highest for a decade ... the Government's opponents ... desperately try to obliterate with their election graffiti this evidence of economic success' (*Daily Mail*, 1 June 1987). The statement may be true, but no documented evidence is quoted, just a vague reference to 'new orders'. The idea of a common economic identity is carried by the phrase 'our factories', which perhaps suggests they belong to everyone. One of the ideological justifications for privatisation was the creation of a wider base of shareholders, and the *Daily Mail* seems to be drawing on that idea.

One of the features of the 1987 general election campaign was that the government offered very little in the way of positive ideas, mainly attacking those put forward by the Labour Party. Even the pro-Conservative newspaper *The Times*, 10 June 1987, commented on the eve of polling that the government party had not presented a clear campaign theme. The analysts David Butler and Dennis Kavanagh have observed of the opinion polls: 'Every poll showed that the NHS was Labour's strongest, and the Conservatives' weakest, issue.'[45] A major consideration in the efficiency of the National Health Service is its financing, which is related to the government's overall economic strategy of curtailing its spending.

In the week of the ballot there were further media attacks on the implications of Labour policies:

Labour tax plan means basic 32p rate

Kinnock will have to raise the standard tax rate to 32p – an extra 5p – to pay for all his promises.

(Gordon Greig, *Daily Mail*, 8 June 1987).

As voting day approached, however, it was not necessarily this financial scare-mongering that caused the Conservatives to lead in the opinion polls. The *Observer* of 7 June 1983 reiterated the problem of divisions within the opposition, blaming those for Thatcher's dominant position despite her perceived lack of positive policies. In this instance it was not so much divisions within Labour, although they had not entirely been overcome, as the fact that the Alliance was likely to take some of the anti-Conservative votes from Labour. The article referred to above regretted the first-past-the-post system of elections in which a party could be comfortably elected without gaining a majority of votes.

The concluding feature of the Conservatives' rather negative strategy has been summarised by Butler and Kavanagh: 'In the final days there was an unprecedented volume of press advertising. The Conservatives spent £2m using all the main newspapers except the *Daily Mirror*.'[46] A representative example of the kind of advertisement can be seen in the full-page message carried on 10 June 1987:

BRITAIN

IS GREAT

AGAIN,

DON'T LET

LABOUR

WRECK IT.

This is partly a reference to Thatcher's successful visit to the USSR less than three months earlier. The greatness is in world affairs rather than economic achievement. In an election in which the opposition offered some kind of hope for a better future, and the out-going government played on fear of what Labour might do if elected, the latter won a large parliamentary majority of 102 seats, and considered it had a mandate to continue the policies it had not defended.

Only four months after this election the reality behind the *Daily Mail's* economic optimism broke through in the Stock Exchange crash that saw a virtual overnight fall of 24 per cent in the overall value of shares. The paradox of the market economy was illustrated by two facts discussed on 24 October 1987, immediately after the financial disaster, by *The Economist*. One factor was that the recession of 1982 had been the worst for fifty years, whilst another was that from 1982 to 1987 Stock Market values rose quickly, making 'many people rich'. One of the problems in understanding why many people became rich in the wake of a disastrous recession, and then suffered financial loss when share values fell catastrophically, because they were based on false economic assumptions, is that 'many' and 'rich' are relative terms. The four or five million people who bought privatisation shares at cheap prices made up to 50 per cent profit in a few weeks, and those, lesser numbers, who played the stock market when prices were rising – partly gaining impetus from the privatisation sell-offs – after 1982 made some money with little effort. But those two or three million people probably made only a few thousand pounds. They did not really become rich, just a little better off. Only the really rich, who had the capital to begin with, became noticably richer. Simultaneously two or three million people who were made unemployed became very much poorer.

13. Thatcher's Major Defeat

Perhaps the single most important event in Britain between the general elections of 1987 and 1992 was the Conservative Party's replacement of

Thatcher by John Major as its leader, and therefore as prime minister, in November 1990. It was an extremely dramatic event, since Thatcher had created a record in winning three successive general elections, and looked, to a large section of the general public, to hold an impregnable, unassailable position as party leader. However, there were a number of matters on which she faced opposition from important people within the government's own ranks.

There was conflict over Britain's relationship to the European Community (EC). Britain was a full member, and yet rejected some of the fundamental aspects of the Community. One of these concerned membership of the Exchange Rate Mechanism (ERM), over which Thatcher had public disputes with her Chancellor of the Exchequer, Nigel Lawson. Thatcher tended to be cooler about the integration of Britain into the EC than some of her cabinet, and other important Conservative figures. She had gained a reputation for an autocratic approach to decision-making that excluded senior MPs from full participation, especially if they were likely to dissent from her views in any way. The political journalist Peter Riddell has observed 'the tendency towards authoritarianism',[47] which was a feature of both the style of her government and Thatcher herself.

The Community Charge, or Poll Tax, was a central factor in the overall conflict. The Conservative Party had been theoretically committed for many years to reforming the local rates system, by which local government raised the bulk of its revenue. That was a tax based on property, and as such one of which Conservatives are naturally suspicious. Suggestions of replacing it with a local sales tax, or income tax, were turned down in favour of the policy Thatcher herself supported. Despite the government's attempts to refer to the new scheme as the Community Charge, its official designation, even the Conservative press referred to it by the common term Poll Tax (literally, a tax on heads). Even the concept itself caused disarray amongst Conservatives. When the Bill introducing it passed through Parliament, in December 1987, the government's majority was only 72, although the election six months earlier had provided Thatcher with a 102-seat majority. Amongst those who did not vote with the government were some senior voices and former cabinet ministers. These included the former prime minister Edward Heath, and Michael Heseltine who subsequently led the challenge to Thatcher's supremacy.

Poll Tax was introduced in Scotland in 1989, and the rest of Britain in 1990. It caused a much greater furore, created a much broader popular opposition, than the government had anticipated. Local councils found it expensive and difficult to collect, in addition to which, the government's original calculations of its likely rate were incorrect. These factors meant the tax was much higher than had been predicted, and since most people paid the same sum (there was a lower rate for people on very low incomes) it was extremely inequitable, unequal and unfair, falling proportionately hardest on groups just above the lowest levels of income.

On the last day of March 1991 a huge anti-Poll Tax rally was held which led to scenes of great violence: 'the most serious rioting in Central London of this century'.[48] The violence was symptomatic of the vehemence, the extremely strong feelings, that had been unleashed by the Poll Tax. As the political commentator Alan Watkins has chronicled, it was not simply left-wing urban radicals who opposed Thatcher's local revenue policy: 'the Conservative shires were planning to overspend ... 18 Conservative councillors in West Oxfordshire resigned ... 200 demonstrated outside the Shire Hall, Taunton. ... Most seriously of all, there was rioting in Tunbridge Wells. The world was being turned upside down.'[49] The general fall in the popularity of the government in opinion polls was attributed, at least in part, to disaffection among traditional Conservative supporters. In Tunbridge Wells, for example, the Conservatives had registered almost 60 per cent of the votes in the 1987 election, and it was considered part of the Tory heartlands. Such internal strife is critical for any party, as Labour had discovered at great cost.

The unpopularity of the Poll Tax, and the effect that had on the government's overall standing amongst voters, was by no means the only issue in November 1990 when Thatcher's leadership was formally challenged in a ballot of Tory MPs. But it had split the party to some extent, and had created anxiety for some MPs that their parliamentary seats would be in danger in a general election if government popularity did not improve. In the complex two-stage contest, Thatcher lost to Heseltine in the first campaign, and had little alternative but to resign as party leader and prime minister.

The egocentric tendencies that made Thatcher such an unpopular prime minister, most of the time with some people and eventually with even fervent Conservatives, were revealed in her recollection of her fall from power. She retained scathing opinions of Michael Heseltine and Geoffrey Howe, both of whom had been members of her cabinets, and who were the two main initial opponents in the challenge to her leadership. Howe had held the important post of Foreign Secretary, and therefore had worked very closely with Thatcher. His resignation speech began the challenge, and Thatcher's account of it is bitter: 'Geoffrey's speech was a powerful Commons performance ... its real purpose ... was to damage me. It was ... poisonous. His long suppressed rancour gave Geoffrey's words more force than he had ever managed before. ... Howe from this point on would be remembered ... for this final act of bile and treachery.'[50] This implies that all Howe's previous speeches, and he was a politician of long experience and high-standing, had been inferior and unforceful, and all his previous achievements would be forgotten. The phrase 'bile and treachery' to describe a speech of honest – even if it were wrong – criticism, displays an almost megalomaniac personality ill-suited to a prime minister. This is also unconsciously revealed in Thatcher's reaction to the events in the House of Commons: 'If the world was listening to him, it was watching me.'[51] Anyone in a position of power, whether in a nation or in a tiny institution, who sees themselves as incapable of error and at the very centre of the universe, is obviously dangerous. The Conservatives had no real choice but to depose her, and in the second stage of electing a new party leader the ultimate winner was John Major, and he became prime minister.

14. The 1990s: A One-Party State?

Thatcher had won the general election of 1987 to remain as prime minister, Major had been appointed to the position by a near-majority of his fellow Conservative MPs. Throughout the late summer and autumn of 1991 there was speculation that he would call a general election to confirm his power. The government, however, was not going through a happy time, with the economy again in deep distress, and Major put off the decision for almost as long as he could. The election was eventually held in April 1992, only two months before it would have been constitutionally necessary.

The Budget was again used to make an appeal to voters, with many commentators linking its emphasis on economic recovery with the forthcoming election campaign. Butler and Kavanagh, looking back, observed: 'On tax the thrust of the Conservative message moved from the effect on take-home pay to the claim that lower taxes would speed recovery: vote for your pocket and do the economy a favour.'[52] Unemployment continued to be very bad, and the number of bankruptcies extremely high. Even so, the one Labour-supporting tabloid proclaimed: 'The state of the National Health Service has become the central issue of the election campaign' (Jill Palmer in the *Daily Mirror*, 1 April 1992). The opinion polls had begun by showing Labour with a popularity lead, but became increasingly uncertain. The *Independent on Sunday*, 5 April 1992, for example, was very unusual in forecasting a Conservative defeat.

Despite that paper's prediction most polls showed increasing doubt about the outcome, and there was speculation that no single party would gain an absolute majority. Right up to polling day itself that expectation was widely held: 'throughout the campaign a hung parliament seemed inevitable'.[53] A 'hung parliament' is one in which no party has a clear overall majority, in which case one of the larger parties would need the support of a smaller, and the most likely pattern predicted was a Labour-led coalition. Kinnock, the Labour leader, talked of a consensus government, and of the possibilities of proportional representation in the future, as the *Independent*, 3 April 1992, reported enthusiastically. Some form of proportional representation, there are several different versions possible, would have been the price of Social and Liberal Democrat cooperation with a Labour prime minister. Ultimately, though, the opposition parties could not agree on a common policy.

As in the previous general election, the Conservative campaign offered little in the nature of positive performance. Poll Tax was to be replaced, and short-term relief from it had been made, although only at the cost of another rise in VAT. The economy remained in profound recession. On the day before voting took place the most popular Conservative newspaper could resort only to the recall of memories of thirteen years previously, with the help of old photographs:

LEST WE FORGET

First-time voters won't remember these shocking scenes. They happened in the late 70s – and they were *all* the fault of the last Labour government: violent flying pickets, the closed schools and hospitals, the endless industrial disputes. Rats roamed mountains of rubbish abandoned by striking binmen. Council workers refused to bury the dead.

(*Sun*, 8 April 1992)

Once again, although this is ostensibly, on the surface, addressed to 'First-time voters', the paper is simply playing on the possibility of a widespread, and perhaps largely mythical, fear of the bad old days. The headline deliberately evokes the language of war memorials. It is an emotive echo of political warfare.

On polling day, 9 April 1992, Labour attempted to open up the main issues through advertisements in several newspapers:

**Vote today
to rebuild
the
economy**

and

**Vote today
to save the
NHS**

The issues were linked through the promised policy: 'Labour will end the recession this year with a £1 billion Economic Recovery Package'.

By the time the booths opened, the *Daily Mirror* had moved its stance from the NHS in particular to the economy in general. Defining 'the priorities of the whole country', the paper declared: 'Top of the list are measures which will get Britain back to work. Taking steps to end the human waste of the Tory years. Putting an end to an era in which grown men and women have been reduced to tears because they could no longer provide for their families' (9 April 1992).

If the nation had to choose between fear of what Labour might do, and the hope for the future carried in its promises, the former proved the stronger again. The Conservative Party won a 17-seat overall majority. This was very much reduced from the previous general election, but nevertheless gave a working control over the House of Commons. One reaction to defeat was to claim that Major had 'based his appeal on the selfishness of the electorate' (*Daily Mirror*, 11 April 1992). One response to victory was self-praise: 'Triumphant Tory MPs queued yesterday to say "Thank You My Sun" for helping John Major back in to Number 10' (John Kay, *Sun*, 11 April 1992). More thoughtful responses were concerned with the fact that the government had begun the campaign behind Labour in the opinion polls, partly as a result of the serious economic recession, yet even in those circumstances the Labour Party had failed to win. It was felt by some open-minded analysts that the cause of Labour's defeat, when all the omens appeared to be in its favour, was the party's failure to present itself as a real potential government. This view was strongly put foward by, in particular, the *Independent* on 10 April 1992. The immediate effect of defeat was the replacement of Kinnock with John Smith as leader of the Labour Party. However, although leaders are important the problem is clearly more profound.

The concern is not merely for the Labour Party, but the country, and its political life, as a whole. Britain has undergone nearly two decades of virtual one-party rule. Many politically non-aligned observers see this as a matter for anxiety. It is not necessarily a healthy democratic state.

This is perhaps illustrated by the fact that, as in 1987, the government got into a major economic and financial crisis within months of winning the election. In September 1992 Britain withdrew from the European Exchange Rate Mechanism (ERM), membership of which had caused fundamental disagreement between Thatcher and her Chancellor three years earlier. It was not a clean-cut decision, being accompanied by ricocheting interest rates and an official devaluation of sterling. It was generally presented in uncompromising terms as a defeat for Lamont, the Chancellor of the Exchequer, specifically, and as marking the collapse of the Conservative's whole economic policy.

Single-party rule over a long period does not necessarily lead to competence, and although that factor is partly a matter of political judgement or faith, it has not led to widespread confidence amongst the populace. On 23 February 1993, just under a year after the last Conservative victory, the results of a Gallup Poll showed that 49 per cent of Britons said they would emigrate if they could. There were many, and complex, reasons why this was the case: a long period of high unemployment, a record number of bankruptcies, an accelerating crime rate, increasing homelessness, a feeling that the National Health Service in particular, and the Welfare State in general, is being dismantled, may all be contributory factors. All have at least some relationship to the economic situation, and that perhaps suggests money alone, ultimately, cannot make the world go round. Something more is needed if the high hopes, ambitions and aspirations that once abounded are ever to be permanently achieved.

Chapter 3 'Who Governs Britain?'

Formally the government governs Britain, of course – and more specifically the prime minister. Nevertheless it is not rule without opposition, and as Thatcher's career illustrates even 10 Downing Street is not entirely a sanctuary from enemies. Although the centre of political argument since 1945 has been between the Conservative and Labour Parties, challenges to governments, and conflicts arising from such actions, are not confined to that duality, or even to the parliamentary processes. This chapter explores challenges to the dual-party system, and to the power of the Westminster Parliament.

1. Breaking the Mould of Tyranny?

In 1960 there were only 7 out of 630 Members of Parliament who did not represent either of the two main parties. In the 1964 general election 9 Liberal Party candidates won seats. It was not until 1974 that dual-party government was seriously challenged. In the October election of that year Labour won 42 more seats than the Conservatives, but 39 MPs represented other parties. The largest single group of those were 13 Liberals. Because of the smallness of Labour's overall majority the Liberals, on occasions, had a key role in maintaining or disrupting the government's power. The balance was so fine that it gave rise in 1977 to an official agreement between the Labour and Liberal Parties. The Lib–Lab Pact, as it was known, failed before the 1979 election, but the clear Conservative majority following that event would have made it irrelevant anyway. Its main defect was that the Liberal Party originally wanted the government to agree to a proportional representation method of voting, in exchange for its support. The Labour Party, however, would not agree to that because it would have undermined its own power at a time it felt confident about the existing election system. One Labour view of the Pact has been recorded by Alistair Michie and Simon Hoggart: 'one of [prime minister]

Callaghan's closer aides was asked if he thought that the Government had got a good deal from the Liberals. He thought for a moment, then said "We took them to the cleaners!"[1] Of course, the report may not be strictly accurate, though the fact that it was recorded close to the events, and the use of a currently popular slang term, tend to give it a flavour of truth. It does seem that any attempt at genuine three-party politics was doomed to failure by the one-sided nature of the experiment.

However, the idea that parliamentary democracy need not necessarily be based around two parties took root. The former Labour cabinet minister Roy Jenkins spoke, in a Richard Dimbleby lecture on BBC1, of the need for a strong centrist grouping, in order to overcome 'what I increasingly regard as the constricting rigidity – almost tyranny – of the present party system' (*The Listener*, 29 November 1979). Jenkins went on to attack two aspects of the 'system', its 'content' and its 'institutions': 'we must try to lengthen our perspective and escape from the tyranny of the belief, against all the evidence, that one government can make or break us. ... One major disadvantage of excessive political partisanship is that it fosters precisely the sort of industrial mood which is rapidly turning Britain into a manufacturing desert.... This ... is an unashamed plea for the strengthening of the political centre ... the case for proportional representation is overwhelming' (ibid.). Jenkins was speaking as a prominent member of the Labour Party a few months after Thatcher's first electoral victory. No one saw, at that time, a series of Conservative governments. It was a bold statement, against the party's official line, using powerful terms such as 'tyranny' to describe the prevailing system. It did not make Jenkins popular, but it did appeal to a number of his colleagues.

Early in 1981 the Social Democratic Party was formed around prominent, disenchanted Labour figures. They quickly became known as the gang of four: David Owen, Shirley Williams, William Rodgers and Roy Jenkins. Owen, to take one example, was a member of the shadow cabinet, the Opposition's prospective cabinet, who became increasingly disillusioned with the Labour Party. In his autobiography he emphasised the extent to which he saw left-wing extremist groups trying to take over the party: 'Each of these groups, to a greater or lesser degree, lived in its own world of purist extremism.'[2] Later, he saw the conflict within the Labour Party intensifying: 'The shaky position of the Labour moderates, backed into a corner, was being constantly demonstrated',[3] and that reached a point at which the only solution appeared to be to leave, and organise something radically different.

The opening point of the launch statement of the Social Democratic Party, made on 26 March 1981 was:

Breaking the mould

Britain needs a reformed and liberated political system without the pointless conflict, the dogma, the violent lurches of policy and the class antagonisms that the two old parties have fostered.[4]

This illustrates a different concern from the ones that drove Owen from the Labour Party. In that case the 'moderates' were being overcome by the 'extremists', but the new party saw both Labour and Conservatives as fostering 'conflict', 'dogma' and 'antagonisms'. The solution to this problem, point two of the launch statement, was to be a new system of electing MPs: 'We need a sensible system of proportional representation in which every vote really counts.'[5]

There was much talk of breaking the mould of British politics, offering an alternative to both Labour and Conservative disenchanted former supporters. The new party quickly had a success, Williams winning a by-election at Crosby by over 5,000 votes in a constituency considered a safe Conservative seat, having had a Conservative majority of 19,000 two years earlier. A new dawn seemed to have been born, and the *Guardian* of 28 November 1981, especially, saw it as a rejection by the voters of left-wing fanaticism and right-wing dogmatists.

In 1983 the Social Democratic and Liberal Parties reached an agreement not to contest the same seats and thereby split potential centrist votes. Apart from being opposed to the two main parties, however, the SDP/Liberal Alliance did not have a strongly agreed manifesto. In fact they remained disunited on a number of fundamental issues. In the 1983 general election the Alliance won only 23 seats – 17 Liberal, 6 SDP – hardly the breaking of any moulds. Overall actual voting figures – rarely accurately reflected in parliamentary power – show that the Conservative and Liberal Parties each received a not dissimilar number of votes in 1983 as in 1979, whilst Labour lost about three million, and the SDP polled around three and a half million. It is not possible to draw too neat a conclusion that most SDP votes in that ballot were gained from former Labour supporters, but a general tendency is certainly evident.

The electoral system did not help the Alliance, and appears to be against the emergence of any strong third parliamentary force. In 1983 the Conservatives gained an enormous majority in the House of Commons with less than 40 per cent of the enfranchised population voting for them. Of the votes actually cast, the Alliance gained over 25 per cent, and Labour less than 28 per cent, less than a million votes separating them, yet Labour finished with 209 MPs against the Alliance's 23. Only in the 1990s, after a series of electoral defeats under this system, did the Labour Party begin to take notions of proportional representation seriously – even so, rather half-heartedly. In the 1970s and 1980s they still thought they could benefit from a first-past-the-post procedure.

By the 1987 general election the Alliance had not resolved the differences between the Liberals and SDP, and its performance was similar to that in the previous ballot. In 1989, after extremely bitter, acrimonious, conflict the SDP split into two groups. The smaller part virtually disappeared from national political life, the larger element merged with the Liberal Party to become the new Liberal Democratic Party. In the 1992 general election it polled nearly six million votes, about 18 per cent, but won only 20 seats, even less than the old Alliance in 1987. The attempt to break the mould of two-party politics had not succeeded, except in the ironic sense that the Conservatives and their supporters appeared to have effectively transformed Britain into a single-party State.

2. Rampant Regionalism: Wales and Scotland

Another feature of British life and politics since the 1960s has been the growing awareness, in some regions, of the amount of power concentrated in London in particular, and perhaps the south-east of England in general. English regionalism has its own flavour, but here I shall explore Welsh and Scottish attempts to wrest political and economic power from London. Unlike the Alliance, the nationalist parties of Wales and Scotland were not concerned with challenging the dual-party system. Realistically they would always be too small to do so. Their purpose in gaining MPs within Parliament was to enable them to attain more power for, and in, Wales and Scotland.

The Welsh nationalist party, Plaid Cymru, had no MPs until it won a by-election in 1966. That was to many people a shock event, the previous Labour majority of over 9,000 votes being turned into a Plaid Cymru victory of more than 2,000. This upsurge of nationalist feeling caused a great deal of consternation, worried concern, amongst Labour government ministers. In the February 1974 general election two Nationalists were elected, and the number has varied between two and three since. Two prominent aspects of Welsh nationalism have been the language, and the selling of property in Wales to English people for holiday homes. This latter occurrence reflects the depopulation of parts of Wales, which is itself a symptom of severe economic decay, and that is obviously a crucial underlying factor. However, attempts to devolve power to a new Welsh parliament have made little headway. Possibly in part because Wales is something of a divided country, both the Welsh tongue and poverty being more prevalent, common, in mid-Wales and the north, predominantly rural areas, than in the more urban south. Nevertheless the political campaign has gained some recognition for the language, with a degree of official bilingualism being accepted.

In March 1979 a referendum in Wales on the issue of the formal devolution of power, the transfer of power from Westminster to an elected Welsh assembly, resulted in a 4 to 1 majority against self-government. As a great number of people did not vote at all only 11.9 per cent of the electorate voted positively for a separate Welsh parliament. This curtailed serious debate about nationalism for some years.

A referendum on the same subject was held simultaneously in Scotland. An extremely narrow majority – 51.6 per cent – of those voting were in favour of self-government, but since less than two-thirds of the population actually voted the result was by no means a nationalist success. Only 32.9 per cent of the electorate were positively in favour of a Scottish assembly. Although the *Morning Star* managed to see it as a victory for self-determination, announcing: 'The Scottish people have declared for an Assembly' (3 March 1979), it was generally accepted as a serious setback. The following day the *Observer*, not a newspaper hostile to the idea of devolution, the transfer of power to regions, accepted that the mood of Scottish nationalists wavered between disappointed and bitter. Since that defeat the Scottish Nationalist Party (SNP) has maintained a presence in the House of Commons, but by no means at the level for which the party had once hoped.

Nevertheless, the party is still operating, and its central goal has not changed. Roger Levy has expressed that bluntly: 'The constitution of the S.N.P. states simply that the party's aim is "Self government for Scotland".'[6] In 1945 the SNP had won a by-election and had for a short time a solitary MP; however that seat was later lost. A 1967 by-election victory at Hamilton, which had been considered a very safe Labour seat was, therefore, a shock even for the victors. A Labour majority of over 16,000 at the general election of the previous year was overturned, with both that party and the Conservatives losing about an equal number of votes to the SNP. The new MP, Winifred Ewing, said, 'Hamilton has made history for

Scotland tonight.' An eye-witness described the ensuing scenes: 'the SNP's election rooms had been taken over by hundreds of members and supporters and the rejoicing went on there throughout the night'.[7]

The SNP's ascendancy was then reflected in numerous local government election victories. According to Morgan these ironically worked against the party, 'because of the relative ineptitude of Scottish Nationalist councillors in the business of local government'.[8] Nevertheless in the February 1974 general election 7 SNP candidates won seats, and that number increased to 11 in the October ballot. That intensified the demands for devolution, partly fuelled by the development of the North Sea oil industry. The idea that oil revenue should belong to Scotland helped nationalism, but paradoxically the actual economic, material wealth the industry created in the country tended to undermine a militancy that had been partially related to financial deprivation (as in Wales). In any event, by 1979 the referendum worked against the nationalists, and in the general election of that year only 2 SNP candidates were elected. Even the subsequent economic recession did not revive the party's fortunes, and in 1987 it won only 3 seats, a disappointing performance that continued into the 1990s.

Regionalism, and its most overt form, nationalism, remain important concepts in Britain. But the idea in the 1970s that the United Kingdom was becoming disunited, was about to fragment as a constitutional entity, seemed by the early 1990s to have faded somewhat. Concessions, such as those on language, and the blurring of a sharp north/south economic line, by the recession of the century's last decade striking harder in the previously affluent south, have served to diminish the force of regionalism. It has not, however, disappeared and future events may cause it to emerge again. For instance, on 30 June 1994 a by-election in the Scottish constituency of Monkton saw a Labour majority that had been over 16,000 in 1992 reduced to less than 2,000 by the SNP candidate, who came second in the poll. Labour retained the seat, but it changed from being considered safe, to one thought as marginal, and vulnerable to Nationalist ambitions. The prime minister at Westminster continues to govern, but should not become complacent about that.

3.   The Irish Dimension

In a way Northern Ireland is a region of Britain, and its problems could be categorised as a form of regionalism. The issues, though, have been more complex, the area more sharply divided within itself than is any other British region. There are 17 MPs representing specifically Northern Ireland political groupings, but that is not the fundamental issue.

Northern Ireland, or Ulster, was created as a political entity within Great Britain in 1921, when southern Ireland became independent as the Republic of Ireland, or Eire. Since that partition there has remained a southern claim that Ireland should be united as a country, but the Republic is overwhelmingly Roman Catholic, whilst two-thirds of the North is Protestant. Religion here is not just a matter of forms of worship or belief, although they can be the cause of bloodshed without other factors, but is integrally compounded with political and economic matters. Many Northern Catholics feel they are discriminated against in jobs, housing and other basic areas of life. Many Protestants feel a threat from the south, and fear a united Ireland would be intolerant of their needs.

As always in politics, understanding the perception of the groups is vital. Macfarlane, commenting on a survey carried out, as it happened, in 1968 immediately before the present troubles began, relates 'that three-quarters of Protestants insisted there was no discrimination against Catholics in Ulster, while three-quarters of Catholics insisted that there was, especially in housing and employment'.[9] Under such circumstances disagreements can become irreconcilable conflicts. The political journalist Harold Jackson wrote shortly after the current crisis had begun: 'From the start of the moves towards independence there had been a fundamental contradiction between nationalist aspirations and the economic reality.... The political consequence was inevitable'.[10] That consequence has been, ultimately, violence.

Paradoxically, whilst Welsh and Scottish nationalists were arguing that they needed a separate assembly to solve their countries' problems, Northern Ireland had a government at Stormont which had a degree of independence from Westminster, and it was the nature of that assembly that in part caused the difficulties. Violence erupted in a particularly serious form late in 1968, when radical Civil Rights protests and demonstrations met with fierce conservative opposition. Troops of the British army were sent by the Westminster authorities to maintain a peace between the conflicting groups in August 1969 during ferocious fighting in the two main cities. A typical newspaper headline ran: 'ALL-NIGHT FIRE BOMB BATTLE IN CITY OF HATE' (Gerry Brown and Noel Whitcombe, *Sun*, 13 August 1969). This was an entirely new development in British politics, and few people at that time thought it would become commonplace.

Mainland political opinion had little initial doubt about the causes of the Troubles: 'chief blame for the appalling Londonderry rioting must fall on the fumbling Ulster Government. ... It is they who lost control and thus provided the opportunity for Mr Jack Lynch, Premier of Eire, to make suggestions more provocative than constructive' (*Sun*, 14 August 1969). Lynch was reported as saying 'Don't use British Army' and 'SEND UN TROOPS' (Michael Lake, ibid.). This was understood to imply that Northern Ireland was a foreign country, not part of Britain, not to be policed by British soldiers. The Stormont government was given the burden of blame in the sense that it was effectively abolished in 1972. The Troubles continued, however, and some mainland opinion has believed that the Irish Republic has encouraged Catholic, Republican ambitions to cause trouble in, and eventually annex, the North.

The weekend after the rioting the *Sunday Times* (17 August 1969) concluded, and most commentators agreed, that the main ingredients of the catastrophe were opportunist trouble makers exploiting miscalculations by politicians, and misunderstandings between communities. As time went on it became increasingly difficult to offer simplistic analysis of anything in Northern Ireland, but after more than a quarter of a century of the conflict it is not easy to appreciate how its beginnings were perceived. In fact this newspaper was quite perceptive in comprehending that the government did not fully understand the implications of events. The government's initial response seems, in retrospect, exceptionally naive: 'The intervention of British troops in riot-torn Londonderry is seen strictly as a limited operation by the British Government. ... Last night's orders to the Army were: Restore law and order with all possible speed, then pull out' (James Render, *Sun*, 15 August 1969).

The situation at that time, however, was volatile, changing almost by the hour. The citizens of the main Catholic area of Londonderry initially welcomed the intervention. The headline referring to a particular district of that city: 'BOGSIDE SINGS A WELCOME TO THE TROOPS' (ibid.), was typical. Again it was the *Sunday Times* that recommended caution in the optimism, in case the Catholics changed their perception of the troops, seeing them as oppressors rather than protectors. That is precisely what happened.

Writing of the decision a couple of years later, the prime minister at the time, Wilson, recorded that he decided not to send troops unless the Ulster Assembly asked for them: 'One thing was clear. At any moment there could be a request from Stormont for us to send in the troops to maintain law and order. Jim Callaghan and I considered whether we should propose their intervention and agreed that it would be unwise. But we decided that once the request came, we should meet it.'[11] Wilson thought it was the right action, and was initially welcomed, because in Northern Ireland: 'the police were regarded, not entirely without justification, by the Roman Catholic minority as biased against them ... Catholics ... contrasted the strictly impartial conduct of the British forces with that they regarded as the committed partiality of the Ulster police.' [12] Unfortunately, the longer the army was engaged in the province the more challenges there were to that perception.

Violence became more widespread, and ultimately the army itself was involved in the most widely, and bitterly, remembered episode of the whole early period of the Troubles: Bloody Sunday. A Civil Rights march early in 1972 ended tragically with the shooting of a number of citizens by the troops. As usual in such circumstances, reports have varied, and perceptions of events are more important than claimed facts. Indeed, facts that are absolutely accepted by all groups involved are extremely few. One newspaper the following day carried a front page report from 'Londonderry': 'The people of this city are consumed with horror to-night ... the hospital reports that 12 people have been brought in dead. ... They are all civilians' (*Financial Times*, 31 January 1972). Describing the Civil Rights march and subsequent events the reporter continued:

> the crowd grew in size until it numbered at least 10,000. Other witnesses say that it was 20,000. ... Marching is illegal, and the authorities were determined that it should not continue and that the crowd should be dispersed. There were 1,500 troops on hand, and 500 policemen.
>
> At this point accounts vary. The official Army explanation is as follows:
>
> The hooligan element turned down side streets, managed to outflank the leaders of the march and confronted the soldiers at the barricades. They threw stones, milk bottles, iron bars and, indeed, anything they could lay their hands on. ... At one stage, some CS gas grenades were also thrown at the troops.
>
> The Army forced the crowd to retreat with tear gas and water canon. Then ... advanced in front of the barricades and started making arrests. About 50 people were held.
>
> Meanwhile, the Army version continues, gunmen opened fire from the rubble at the base of the Rossville Flats, and soldiers returned the fire. Mr Michael Canavan, chairman of the Derry Citizens Central Council, explaints [sic] it differently.
>
> He says that the Army opened fire indiscriminately, with hundreds of people in the streets, ad [sic] before there had been any other shots. ...
>
> The Bogsiders even allege that the Army fired on Red Cross personnel. ...
> The hours that followed were poisoned with rumour and counter-rumour.
>
> (John Graham, ibid.)

This report brings out clearly the gap between the perceptions of events. On one hand the army claim it faced a quasi-military attack from 'gas grenades' and 'gunmen', whilst the citizens 'even allege that the Army fired on Red Cross personnel', who would obviously be non-combatants and represent no threat to the soldiers. The moment of battle is always fraught, with judgement and subsequent memory often distorted.

The emotion generated by the incident was not confined to Northern Ireland. On the following day the *Financial Times* carried another front-page report:

Violence in the Commons

> Amid extraordinary scenes of uproar in the Commons yesterday Miss Berna-dette Devlin (Ind., Mid Ulster) rushed across the floor of the Chamber and attacked Mr Reginald Maudling, the Home Secretary, by hitting him in the face, scratching him, and tearing at his hair. . . . For a further few moments, as Miss Devlin was being pulled away, a confused fracas developed in the middle of the floor of the Chamber.
>
> (John Hunt, *Financial Times*, 1 February 1972)

Devlin had also called Maudling a 'murdering hypocrite' (*Hansard*, 31 January 1972), a phrase that was not considered correct Parliamentary language, and one that did not defuse the emotional situation. This kind of scene is very rare in the British Parliament, illustrating the rawness of the emotions provoked by Bloody Sunday. The whole episode evoked greater violence in Northern Ireland, and contributed to the further spread of IRA (Irish Republican Army) activity to the mainland. Until this time Northern Ireland had its own political assembly with a degree of self-government, but it was in the extreme crisis following this episode that Heath, as British prime minister, suspended that organisation so that the region was governed directly and unambiguously from London under a Secretary for Northern Ireland.

This hardened attitudes within the province, Catholics tending to interpret it as an imposition of foreign military rule, and Ulster Pro-testants as an undermining of their status. When in 1973 the British embassy in Dublin was burnt to the ground some Northern Protestants saw it as an act of intimidation that reflected the covert ambitions of the Republican government of the south. In the North both militant Catholics and Protestants responded with increased violence against one another, and the IRA carried the battle onto the mainland.

Within a few months of Bloody Sunday the *Daily Telegraph* (14 July 1972) was commenting on the anarchic establishment of no-go areas controlled by terrorists, on murder becoming commonplace and large-scale terrorist bombing operations. The specific turning point was widely seen to be 30 January 1972. By then the Conservative Heath had become prime minister, and Andrew Roth thought: ' "Bloody Sunday" suddenly transformed British troops in Northern Ireland into the traditional villains of Irish history. It also brought tumbling the slow-moving initiative that Heath and his Ministers had long been trying to get off the ground.'[13]

Such initiatives have been tried fairly regularly. At the beginning of the Thatcher era, for instance, her Secretary of State for Northern Ireland, Humphrey Atkins, said in the House of Commons: 'all the political parties are on record as wanting a transfer of power to elected representatives in Northern Ireland . . . so the Government's view is that it will be right to propose arrangements for renewed political life in the Province. . . . We need to search for something which . . . would be regarded by enough people in all parts of the community as a step forward' (*Hansard*, 29 November 1979). Such attempts to find political resolutions have been drowned in a sea of violence. Another initiative launched in a blaze of publicity, the Anglo-Irish Agreement of 1985, sought to create a Council of Ireland in conjunction with the Republic's government which would, in theory, have recognised the rights of Northern Catholics whilst safeguarding the interests of Protestants. It also, for many reasons, failed to resolve the problems.

The general feeling in mainland Britain seems to have hovered between horror and despair. In so far as Ireland is a separate island it can appear to be someone else's problem, but there are a great many Irish, and people with Irish ancestry on the mainland, particularly in England, and as the IRA have carried the war across the Irish Sea, it is not an issue that can simply be forgotten. Even after the current crisis has been resolved the underlying bitterness and fears will not disappear overnight, and any long-term resolution will have to take account of them if they are not to recur at some point in the future.

There have been very many incidents of terrorism in England during the century's last three decades, some against specific individuals, others indiscriminate in their effects. None will be simply forgotten. Just two examples of the former are the assassination of Airey Neave shortly before the general election of 1979, and the Brighton hotel bomb of 1984.

Neave was a prominent Conservative MP, and close associate of the Conservative leader, Thatcher. His death by a car-bomb caused widespread alarm, partly because until then it had been felt that high-profile potential terrorist targets in England were well protected by the security forces. That faith was shaken to an even greater degree in October 1984 when a bomb was exploded at the Brighton hotel in which virtually the whole cabinet was staying during a Conservative Party conference. In all five people died, although none of the central political targets, which included the prime minister, were killed. Again it caused great alarm about the effectiveness of the security forces, but as perhaps in 1979 the propaganda effect probably aided Conservative popularity in Britain as a whole.

This is illustrated by the response of the daily Labour-supporting newspaper, which carried the simple headline 'MURDER' (*Daily Mirror*, 13 October 1984) over photographs of Thatcher and the devastated hotel. It reported: 'THE IRA SAID YESTERDAY: "Today we were unlucky, but remember we have only to be lucky once."' The paper was not in sympathy with this statement, and in its leader column announced: 'The carefree days before terrorism have long gone. . . . Many people, from Mrs Thatcher down, showed great personal courage' (ibid.). The danger the prime minister was unconsciously in gave her heroic status: 'Maggie sixty seconds from death. . . . Defiant Thatcher warns that terrorism will never win' (ibid). In fact, even in an anti-Thatcher paper, she became a symbol of the whole of Britain standing defiantly against terrorism.

Her response was widely reported: 'It was an attempt not only to disrupt and terminate our conference, it was an attempt to cripple Her Majesty's democratically elected government.' In this speech Thatcher appealed for the sympathy and support not only of Conservatives, whose representatives had been personally attacked at 'our conference', but in addition to everyone who believed in democracy and the value of a 'democratically elected government'. Because that government belongs to 'Her Majesty' and Thatcher speaks as its head there is even a sense in which the prime minister is speaking for, and representing, the Queen herself. The effect of the bombing was to strengthen support for the government's attitudes and policies.

Norman Tebbit, a cabinet minister, who was badly injured, as was his wife, in the bombing, later testified to the backlash publicity effect of the terrorism: 'television pictures of our rescue had gone around the world evoking a wave of sympathy, and thousands of letters from heads of state and ordinary people alike – not least from the Republic of Ireland – and from incredible numbers of children'.[14] Similarly, although the indiscriminate attacks by terrorist groups did gain them, and the issue, enormous publicity, they also probably created a backlash of public opinion against any political solution that might seem to favour the perpetrators of violence. Again, there have been numerous such incidents, and I will mention only a couple to give a feeling of the atmosphere.

Relatively early in the period of the Troubles, in 1974, bombs exploded in two crowded public houses in Birmingham. Twenty-one people died, and 162 were injured; reports emphasised the horror, the arbitrary nature of the action and its consequences. Survivors were typically quoted in terms of: 'There were mutilated bodies everywhere ... there was blood and limbs everywhere' (Ann Buchanan *et al.*, *Sun*, 23 November 1974). The same newspaper reported that subsequently, 'A wave of anger and hatred swept the Midlands ... hundreds of workers demanded the return of hanging' (ibid.). A photograph of marching workers with appropriate placards supported the report.

Similar episodes of violence were occurring in Northern Ireland, but the British media as a whole gave much fuller coverage to mainland attacks. The lack of progress in resolving the problems is indicated by the fact that almost twenty years later explosions were still occurring in purely civilian areas. In March 1993 two bombs placed in a shopping district of Warrington in Lancashire exploded, killing two boys, aged 3 and 12. The media widely, and almost universally, reported the event as an 'atrocity'. Reports concentrated on how the townspeople as a whole reacted against the incident, describing how flowers and cards of condolence and memory had the day after been heaped on the spot. One card read: 'May God forgive them, because we can't'.

The fact that the victims were not only innocent shoppers, but children, created an intensely emotional response. A report of the funeral of one of the victims emphasised the involvement of the whole community, expressing a general feeling on a black-bordered front page:

NO MORE BLOOD

NO MORE TEARS

There was no bitterness, no anger. Just a quiet dignity and awesome courage ... the latest bloodied medal on the chest of Ireland's blackhearted killers. Today the other innocent victim of the IRA's Warrington bomb ... will be buried.

Tomorrow their broken bodies must be the stepping stones to peace.

Throughout Britain and Ireland the voices of ordinary people call out in anger and disgust. They share one simple message, an anthem that must grow and become irresistible.

(Daily Mirror, 26 March 1993)

The same edition reported the formation of a new Irish peace movement, quoting the Dublin organiser, Susan McHugh, as saying: 'I now hope everyone in Ireland will come out and show their unequivocal disapproval. ... There must be compromise. There must be some solution to stop the violence. ... The terrorists do not represent us. ... The time for reconciliation is here' (Patrick Mulchrone, ibid.). Peace rallies in Dublin and Warrington were attended by tens of thousands of people.

In the following month, however, another enormous bomb was detonated in London, creating a crater fifteen feet deep and causing one death and injuring more than 40 people. Reports generally agreed that it was only a matter of luck that the casualty toll was not far greater. They also made a direct connection between that bombing and the IRA's rejection of the message of the peace rallies. Later in the year, just as formal peace negotiations were to begin there was another outbreak of intense political violence, with 14 people being murdered and more than 60 injured in a single week in Ulster. The connection of timing between official attempts to find a solution and increased para-military murders hardly seemed to be a coincidence at the time.

After the murders of over three thousand people, the premiers of Britain and the Irish Republic produced a 'Joint Declaration' to form a basis for:

PEACE AT LAST

Irish Premier Albert Reynolds ... believes the declaration will provide peace by Christmas ... a permanent end to nearly 25 years of bloodshed.
(John Williams, *Daily Mirror*, 15 December 1993)

However, the murders continued and more cautious responses – typified by that in the *Independent* of the same day – stressing the potential for peace, rather than its achievement, appeared to have greater immediate realism. The three main strands of the agreement were: allowing the political wing of the IRA into negotiations after a period of non-violence; removal from the Republic's constitution of its outright territorial claims on Ulster; a concept of political self-determination for the people of the North.

Since the present Troubles date back to 1968 – and the fundamental issues perhaps to the sixteenth century – few Northern Ireland people under middle-age have any clear memory, if any at all, of a time of peace. For an increasing proportion of the population warfare, or fear of it, is the only atmosphere and circumstance they have ever known. It might well be argued that in reality Ulster has been governed by the para-military forces, both Catholic and Protestant, rather than by the London-based Government. In that case the constitutional authority is not defending its power from challenge, but attempting to wrest back a status it lost. This distinction was perceptively, and prophetically, expressed in the *Sunday Times* of 17 August 1969 only a few days after the first troops had arrived in Northern Ireland. In any State faced with terrorism that is a central issue.

David Waddington concludes his academic study of the problem: 'The key lesson ... is that order cannot be coercively imposed, and that some form of political consensus is necessary ... to create a constitutional forum for political discussion involving, amongst others, the paramilitary organisations.' [15] When the IRA announced a 'cessation of military operations' to take effect from 1 September 1994 many people saw it as a chance for immediate salvation, and were disappointed that the Protestant Loyalists of Northern Ireland did not instantly also make a similar gesture, creating a consensus for a 'constitutional forum'. One problem was that less than two months earlier the Dublin government had rejected a suggestion that Article 2 of the Republic's constitution should be amended. This Article claims the 'whole island of Ireland' must be united. The old protestant fear that the London Government had come to a secret deal with Dublin, and the IRA, which would lead to them becoming the minority in a united Republican Ireland emerged as a strong force creating suspicion. Paradoxically, the Loyalists felt the enemy had become the very Government to which they nominally claimed loyalty. Nevertheless, the Loyalists were persuaded to join the ceasefire and, although in an atmosphere of mutual distrust, tentative negotiations did get underway in the following months. By March 1995 the situation was sufficiently hopeful for the Queen to make a well-publicised visit to Ulster, and for the Army to announce a withdrawal of some troops.

4. The Lost Legions: Trade Unions

The question that heads this chapter, although obviously appropriate to the forces discussed so far, was used specifically of the conflict between the trade unions, the National Union of Mineworkers in particular, and the Heath government. Butler and Kavanagh concluded of the February 1974 general election campaign: 'the twin themes of inflation and "who governs" were central'.[16] They recorded that after the Conservatives had lost the election Heath said of the issue 'Who Governs Britain?': 'This question will certainly recur throughout the life of the Parliament and the Party should be neither ashamed of having put it to the electorate in the past nor unready to do so in the future'.[17] Although it is a typically emotive electioneering slogan, trade union power had reached proportions at which the question could appear to be valid to some voters.

Through the 1960s trade union power grew partly because of governments' full-employment economic policies (cf. Chapter 2). With a relatively small pool of unemployed people strike action by trade unionists
could bring firms, and whole industries, to a standstill. The strike threat
was a strong bargaining, some would say blackmailing, tactic. The more
members a union had the more powerful a negotiating position it held,
and the better deals it could achieve the more workers would join. In the
1961 census the total working population was put at just under 25 million,
and trade union membership at virtually 10 million. The size of the
working population did not vary much during the decade, but union
membership had grown to over 11 million by the next census, in 1971. In
fact it kept growing until it peaked at well over 13 million in 1979.

The strike threat was not often a strategy of bluff. In 1961 over 3 million
working days were lost in strikes; by the end of the decade the figure had
risen to over 4 million. In a response to the situation, the Minister for
Employment and Productivity, Barbara Castle, produced a White Paper,
a statement of government intent, or desires, *In Place of Strife* in 1969. As
the title suggests, the intention was to replace an arena of industrial
relations in which conflict was becoming increasingly the norm, with
conditions that lessened strife. Although the proposal strengthened trade
unions in some ways, it also curtailed their powers of action in others –
and those were the areas of proposed legislation that received most focus.
It was considered paradoxical that a Labour government wanted to bring
in laws that a Conservative cabinet of the time would hardly have dared to
think about.

The trade unions felt the government was betraying them; the feelings
of the Labour government's leadership were that union attitudes undermined longer-term economic plans. Castle wrote that her plan recognised
union rights: 'it rejected the idea that strikes were always to be deplored.
... The White Paper ... was first and foremost a charter of trade union
rights'.[18] She was, however, never able to convince the unions, writing
subsequently that the Trades Union Congress (TUC) 'remained deeply
suspicious of any interference in the running of union affairs or any hint
of sanctions against unions. I was soon in difficulties'.[19] Those difficulties
are illustrated by an account by the political commentator Peter Jenkins
of a meeting, during this process, between Wilson, the prime minister,
and the two powerful union leaders Hugh Scanlon and Jack Jones:
'Wilson was enraged at the intransigence and arrogance of the two union
leaders';[20] Wilson is reported to have said 'Get your tanks off my lawn
Hughie!'[21] With about fifty Labour MPs stating they would vote against

any Bill in Parliament that was based on the White Paper, it was not only the unions who were suspicious of the implications of the proposed action. Opposition grew to the extent that Wilson accepted a compromise which in essence was a defeat. An agreement was reached that the TUC would monitor and attempt to regulate strikes. Prophetically sensing the predominant idea of the period, and the title of this chapter, *The Economist* parodied Castle's document, and the ultimate fate of its intentions, by referring to the process as 'In Place of Government' (21 June 1969). This sceptical response was ultimately considered justified, by some people, although not all, as the number of working days lost in strikes virtually doubled during the two following years. By then the Conservative Heath had replaced Wilson as prime minister.

The Conservative government elected in 1970 did pass an Industrial Relations Act in the following year, but it worked more successfully against unofficial strikes – actions taken by workers without official union support, or even against the leadership's decisions – than against formal trade union activity. In fact putting strikers into prison, even when they were technically acting illegally, was not a popular policy. As nearly half the workforce belonged to a trade union it was also a dangerous one in regard to industrial relations, so that the employers' association, the CBI (Confederation of British Industries), was also not happy about it. The CBI's Director-General, Campbell Adamson, subsequently – on 26 February 1974, at the climax of the election campaign – urged its repeal because it was souring industrial relations.

Late in 1971 the government tried to impose a wage-restraint policy, which inevitably led to a major industrial-relations confrontation. In January 1972, in the middle of a hard winter, the NUM began its first national miners' strike since 1926 in support of a pay claim. Many newspapers presented the union as unreasonable, rejecting an offer of conciliation from the Department of Employment, on 7 January 1972, in order to create confrontation. There is, though, usually more than one view of any conflict. The NUM president, Joe Gormley, later recalled his thoughts on the process: 'We weren't negotiating with the right people. The NCB [National Coal Board] were the people chosen to run the coal industry, and to negotiate with the workers in that industry. But they weren't being allowed to exercise those functions. Whatever the Board might say, it was quite clear, almost from the outset, that they were being completely hamstrung by the dictates of the Heath policies.'[22]

The effect of the strike was immediate. Not only was the production of coal stopped, but the use of mass flying pickets – not literally flying, but moving quickly around the country – also prevented the movement of coal stocks. In February the government were looking for a face-saving compromise, which they attempted to achieve through the appointment of a Committee of Inquiry under an independent judge. In the light of its recommendations, that the miners were indeed a special case, the NUM gained a highly advantageous settlement. Just as the Labour government's policy in 1969 had been defeated by concerted and determined trade union action, so too, despite the attempt to hide behind compromise, had the Conservatives' in 1972.

That was an important aspect of the background to the 1973–4 dispute between Heath's government and the NUM mentioned in Chapter 2 as part of the build-up to the February 1974 general election. The atmosphere of industrial warfare was expressed when the NUM made its decision not to accept the original terms it was offered: 'MINERS MAKE IT FIGHT TO FINISH' (Anthony Shrimsley, *Daily Mail*, 22 November 1973). During the course of the strike the prime minister was reported, on 8 February 1974, as claiming that some of the people involved in the dispute were specifically politically motivated, wanting to bring down not just the current government, but any elected government. A sense of desperation and viciousness pervaded the conflict, a feeling there was more at stake than simply the level of a wage increase.

Heath's plea to the electorate to vote for the Conservatives against the power of unions, and the Labour Party with whom they were associated (despite the 1969 shambles), was not successful. The slogan/question 'Who Governs Britain?' implied that the election was a contest between parliamentary democracy and brutish economic/industrial power. But at that time many people had sympathy for the miners, recognising the importance and danger of their work. It was a unique election, held during a major and bitter strike, which came up with a rare result, no party holding an overall clear majority. Labour's Wilson became prime minister and the miner's strike was settled to their satisfaction very quickly. Trade union strength appeared to have triumphed again.

After the October 1974 election had again returned a Labour government without a definite working majority the party and the TUC implemented another agreement. The social contract, or compact, as it was known, gave trade unions concessions in the areas of legislation and industrial policies in return for voluntary wage restraint. However, individual unions were not necessarily bound by TUC decisions, and in a period of rampant inflation felt free to pursue large wage claims. One result was disarray within the labour movement – internally in the Party, between unions and TUC, and between individual unions. The Labour government saw three attempts to impose wage-restraint policies fail, and working days lost through strikes continued to be high, around 10 million in each of the years 1977–8.

The winter of discontent of 1978–9 has already been touched on in the previous chapter. There did appear to be another struggle over who governed Britain, with the social contract well and truly torn up. The number of strike days for 1979 was treble that of the previous years, most of them occurring in the months leading up to the May general election. A transport strike threatened to paralyse the whole country by depriving it of petrol supplies: 'Drivers suffered miles of misery yesterday in a frantic search for petrol. ... But militant Texaco shop stewards, whose wildcat strike and flying pickets have caused the famine, blamed the public for the crisis' (James Lewthwaite and Tom Condon, *Sun*, 8 January 1979). A 'wildcat strike' is simply an unofficial one, not recognised by the union leadership; however, the informal term is very much more emotive than the formal, with its association of viciousness and a predatory nature. In this case the predators are the 'militant ... shop stewards' who have not merely caused 'the famine' (of petrol) but are callous enough to blame 'the public'. It has to be recognised that the *Sun* is the most Tory of newspapers, and the most anti-union, writing emotively of industrial relations. We have, though, also to remember that it is the most widely read paper in Britain, which can both influence and reflect popular opinion.

The same edition reminded readers that an election was constitutionally inevitable sometime that year, and that the 'victims of the current wave of senseless strikes' should take heed of 'Mrs Thatcher's pledge that she will deal sensibly and firmly with trade unions'. The promise 'comes as a ray of sunshine to strike-torn, battered Britain' (ibid.). The Labour prime minister – now James Callaghan, who had taken over from Harold Wilson three years earlier – was also reported as getting tough with the unions: 'Callaghan warned the unions yesterday: Put your house in order over picketing or Labour will lose the next election' (Walter Terry, *Sun*, 18 January 1979). On this occasion the paper saw trade union power as a greater threat than Labour Party power. With Britain in a 'SHUTDOWN' (Peter McHugh and John Kay, *Sun*, 13 January 1979) state, the question Who Governs Britain? had clearly re-emerged. But there is always more than one side to an argument, and the Communist Party daily newspaper presented the unions as victims of government betrayal:

JIM PLAYS THE STRIKE DIRTY

Premier Callaghan last night launched an outrageous attack on the lorry drivers
and on the whole trade union movement.

(Martin Gostwick and Andrew Murray, *Morning Star*, 17 January 1979)

There were shades of the 1926 General Strike in the minds of more than
Communists. A symbol of the venom that had built up between government and unions was the former's threat to use soldiers as emergency
workers: 'Troops were put on "red alert" last night as fury mounted over a
decision by ambulancemen not to man life-and-death services on
Monday. Strike leader Bill Dunn left a shop stewards meeting and said:
"If lives are lost, that is how it must be" ' (Keith Deves, *Sun*, 20 January
1979). The hostile reporting was general in the press, with Dunn's comment being taken out of context. Nevertheless, with icy roads not being
gritted, huge piles of health-endangering rubbish building up in streets,
and shortages of some basic supplies, the mood of anti-unionism was not
entirely confined to the Conservative press. Terms such as anarchy were
in general use to describe the situation.

In effect the government fell two months later when it was defeated on a
vote of confidence in the House of Commons, just as the chaos was
lessening. Just before the general election the Conservative Party capi-
talised on the implicit Who Governs Britain? uncertainty by alleging that
left-wing extremists were about to take control of the Labour Party. The
Guardian reported this, ironically, on International Labour Day (1 May
1979). The argument, no matter how false, that Leftish fanatics, having
failed to gain control of the country through the trade unions, would
achieve power by taking over the Labour Party, made sense to some
people. It is the kind of cross the Labour leadership has had to bear
throughout the twentieth century.

After Thatcher had gained power she began to fulfil her promise, as
reported in the *Sun* (above), to deal 'firmly' with the unions. There were
Acts of Parliament limiting, or curtailing, trade union activity in various
ways in 1980, 1982, 1984 and 1988. Edgar Wilson summarises the cumu-
lative effect of these as: 'to limit secondary picketing and action, curtail the
closed shop, make unions financially liable to damages for strikes, and
require secret ballots before strike action is taken'.[23] In less than a decade
it had become illegal for unions to use flying pickets, to send pickets from
site to site; the behaviour of picket lines was controlled by law; unions
could no longer insist that all workers in a particular employment had to
be union members; unions could be sued by employers for damage to

trade caused by strikes; and no strike could be legally called without a secret ballot of members.

Edgar Wilson has described these actions as a 'vendetta against trade unions'.[24] The political theorist Martin Holmes interprets the initial assault on trade unionism from another perspective than the ideological one put forward by such observers as Edgar Wilson, who is not alone in his interpretation. Holmes wrote: 'The idea that the unions had a role to play in formulating government policy ... was repudiated. ... Thatcher's hostility to union power was part of the legacy from both the Heath period and the 1974–9 Labour government. The Prime Minister was determined that her administration would not be humiliated in the way that events had overtaken the two previous administrations'.[25] This provides a more specifically historically based interpretation, founded on the idea that the central question was Who Governs Britain? We may chose between different perceptions of history and politics, but we do not necessarily have to – there may be truth in the views of both Wilson and Holmes. Understanding the historical context enables us to appreciate the central concerns that motivate action.

In fact it is probably significant that the first Thatcher government did suffer a minor defeat by the NUM. To observers looking back on events that may have seemed a relatively unimportant episode, but it is an interesting example of how the passage of time can change perspectives. When it occurred the miners' victory appeared to be very important. The government announced plans to close 23 pits, the NUM threatened to strike, and the Conservatives, to almost universal amazement, withdrew. The *Guardian* of 19 February 1981 wrote of it in terms of unprecedented high drama, and all the media agreed that the decision was extremely unexpected. The swiftness of the U-turn, after strong and aggressive government statements about the need to curb public spending, caused alarm in Conservative ranks. Thatcher was accused by her own supporters of having retreated. The use of the concept of retreat in that context was revealing, portraying the dispute in military terms, as a physical battle between government and trade union, in which the latter was victorious. There is little doubt that defeat sharpened the government's tactics, and appetite, for any future confrontation with the miners. That event occurred in 1984.

That is often taken as the most momentous event involving trade unions and Thatcher, but just before the confrontation began, the government actually banned trade union membership to staff employed at the Government Communications Headquarters (GCHQ). Workers who were already members of the relevant trade union were forced to resign that basic right in order to stay in employment. The government acted unilaterally, without any consultation with anyone, or constitutional debate. When parliament was informed of the decision, which had already been taken, even the moderate and placid David Owen was roused to anger: 'It affects the fundamental liberties of well over 5,000 of our citizens ... there are other ways of achieving the desirable objectives ... the action has already been taken without any consultation' (*Hansard*, 25 January 1984). Many citizens did indeed lose their 'fundamental liberties', and to some it seemed a grimly ironic way of opening the year Nineteen Eighty-Four in view of George Orwell's novel of that title, in which totalitarianism is attacked for denying 'fundamental liberties'. The reason given for the ban was the possibility of workers at the Headquarters passing secret information to an enemy power. Denis Skinner, speaking in the House of Commons, observed that 'throughout the age all Fascists have used the cloak of national security and national interest to chip away at hard-won liberties and freedoms, especially those affecting the trade unions' (ibid.). He went on to point out that all the famous, or infamous, spies had been former public school boys and graduates of the University of Cambridge, rather than ordinary workers. However, by the mid-1990s the fundamental liberties remain denied.

Historically that denial has been overshadowed by the NUM's strike of March 1984 to March 1985. Any national strike lasting for that length of time, and involving at its peak upwards of 200,000 workers, is a complex episode. Many complete books have been written, and will no doubt be written, on the subject, and here there is space for only an outline discussion. It certainly ended in a government victory, and because of the previous power of the miners, who were seen as the vanguard of the trade union movement, the Conservatives appeared to have won not simply a battle but the whole war with unionism.

The reasons given for the outcome have been numerous: lack of support from other unions and the TUC, the military-like organisation and violent behaviour of the police, the harsh sentences imposed in courts on those strikers and others arrested, media bias against the strikers in reports. In addition, no one has yet convincingly explained why the NUM began a strike in the spring, when demand for coal was going to be at its lowest for the next six months. Half way through the strike a large group of miners formed a breakaway union, the Union of Democratic Mineworkers (UDM), which reveals a serious split within the workers, and a lack of confidence in the competence of the NUM leadership.

The political dimension of the strike has been remarked on by many commentators. The journalist Geoffrey Goodman, whilst noting the differences between the 1984 action and 'the 1926 strike which, for nine days, precipitated a general strike', also claims that 'the parallels ... are quite uncanny'.[26] He adds that it was Thatcher who caused, or precipitated, this crisis in order 'to avenge earlier defeats',[27] so that the government brought its own political dimension into the battle. A former member of the Young Liberals, Peter Hain, has perceived that element too: 'the Thatcherites were less concerned about the *financial* cost of the strike to the public purse than the *political* cost of losing it. It was crucial to their overall political project to alter the balance of power and class forces in Britain'.[28] Clearly events had little connection with mere industrial relations, a relationship between employers and employees. As the government subsidised the coal industry, in the interests of the national economy, it controlled the head of the National Coal Board. Indeed, during the autumn, in the run-up to the strike, the government had appointed Ian MacGregor as chairman of the NCB, a man of whom the authors Martin Adeney and John Lloyd have written 'Privately, he believed unions were an abomination.'[29] There was no conflict between the aims of MacGregor and the prime minister. The dispute was between Thatcherism and unionism over the issue of power: another re-run of the question Who Governs Britain? In this case the answer was unambiguously Thatcher. The miners returned to work having achieved none of their objectives, and the whole trade union movement continued to decline throughout the decade.

It is necessary, though, to realise that Thatcher was not solely anti-union – the government pursued other opponents vigorously too; and the trade union movement continued to be harassed after Thatcher had herself been removed from office. Individuals who were prosecuted through the law courts, such as Clive Ponting, Sarah Tisdall and Peter Wright, amongst others, all of whom were accused during the 1980s, in various ways, of revealing official secrets, or disclosing factual material that showed government representatives had lied on particular occasions, were not trying to gain control of Britain. However, the rigour with which such opposition to government power was attacked does illustrate the determination of the administration to accept no ambiguity about its authority.

Despite the setbacks, the lost legions of trade unionists are not, in the last decade of the century, in fact completely lost. Union membership has fallen – probably largely because of increasing unemployment – almost continuously since the catalyst year of 1979, and the 'winter of discontent' general election that saw the beginning of four successive Conservative administrations. Membership in the early 1990s was less than 40 per cent of the workforce, as opposed to over 50 per cent at its peak in the late 1970s, and by 1990 annual strike days numbered around two million, as against over 29 million in 1979. Nevertheless, looked at from a different perspective, over one third of the workforce still do belong to a trade union, and the early 1990s did see some resurgence of union activity.

Relations between government and workers remained strained. In October 1992 the government suddenly announced the closure of 31 coal mines, and that autocratic act provoked almost universal disapproval. Although the NUM was the organisation most directly affected, a rally in London against the government's policy attracted much wider support. A march stretching for over four miles was reported to contain even Conservative voters who were against the Government's policy on coal-mining. In Parliament the Conservative backbench MP Winston Churchill accused the Party leaders of 'letting down the nation ... [rekindling] anger and outrage' (*Hansard*, 21 October 1992). On the very day of the march the Government appeared to capitulate to the widespread protests, agreeing to a review of its pit-closure programme.

The government, however, were not so easily defeated, and achieved their objective over a period of time through subterfuge, or cunning. A year after those events, British Coal announced its pessimism regarding the future of twelve pits. A number of newspapers reported a mood of having been betrayed among the Conservative MPs who had opposed their leaders, Churchill being particularly vocal in his protestations and recriminations on behalf of the miners and his backbench colleagues. There was a general feeling that the Conservative government was determined to effectively destroy the British coal-mining industry whatever the opposition.

Not all protests, however, were entirely fruitless. After suffering years of political interference in education the majority of teachers decided in 1993 not to carry out the testing of children at the age of fourteen. The government insisted it was necessary, teachers argued that it was anti-educational as it wasted a great deal of time without achieving anything positive. The teachers' boycott of this testing was interpreted by the government as a form of industrial action, and *The Times* of 23 April 1993 reported that the Conservatives were planning to change the law if teachers continued the boycott, to make such action illegal.

This threat occurred against a background of increasing public support for the teachers. A few weeks after the possibility of government intervention was revealed a National Opinion Poll of parents with children aged between 5 and 16 years old showed over half supporting the teachers, and only 27 per cent actually opposing them on the issue. The *Independent* (10 May 1993) observed wryly that the government's publicity campaign, which cost the taxpayers three-quarters of a million pounds, seemed not to have been effective. Teachers, not surprisingly, thought that amount of money spent on advertising a profoundly flawed policy might have been better invested in actual education. Most people seemed to agree that John Patten, the Secretary of State for Education, had not necessarily the most competent judgement in the matter, another poll showing that a mere 19 per cent of those questioned thought he was performing his job well, although it was not until the following year, 1994, that the prime minister removed him from office.

The struggle between government and unions over fundamental liberties was clearly not resolved with Thatcher's dismissal from office. The contemporary Conservative Party in power remains intolerant of any opposition it feels it can crush. On 3 August 1993 even the newspaper most opposed to the teachers, the *Daily Telegraph*, conceded that their action had slowed down the speed of changes in education, and had done so on educational grounds. It is significant that neither of the actions discussed here, essentially conflicts between unions and the Conservative administration, are about mere wages or salaries, the great issues of the 1960s and 1970s. They are issues concerned with the whole economic and social future of Britain.

There can no longer be any doubt that it is not the trade unions who govern Britain. The days of naive power, when union activity could casually bring down a government, thinking that it could deal with the next prime minister in the same way, have certainly passed. However, as the teachers in particular have shown, unions can perform an essential democratic function in linking power and responsibility. At a time when decisions are being made for political reasons, with responsibility for carrying them out being simply passed on to someone else, it is important that the consequences of such a form of government are not ignored. Trade unions and workers have become involved in disputes that are concerned not with today's pay packet, but with their contributions to the future of Britain's quality of life. Teachers, for instance, argue that the power to make decisions about education should rest, at least in part, with the people who have the responsibility for, and specialist knowledge of, education. It is an interesting idea, for whoever governs Britain today will eventually have to hand over to the current younger generation. The future is always becoming the present.

Chapter 4 Battles on the Streets

'I took part in a magnificent rally today. ... It was an exhilarating experience. ... A catalyst has been at work in the past few days and has overwhelmed us all. We did not appreciate the extent to which the closures had got up the nose of many Tories. ... We have all been swamped with letters from our constituents' (*Hansard*, 21 October 1992). The speaker was the Labour MP Denis Skinner, and the rally he was describing to the House of Commons was the mass protest concerning the government's announcement of its intention to close 31 coal mines, the issue discussed towards the end of the previous chapter. In a widely reported speech he had told the protesters the battle would not be won in Parliament, but 'We will win it on the streets.' Although Skinner is considered by many to be a political eccentric, a maverick figure of the Labour left-wing, his views do express an important line of radical direct-action thought, which has become increasingly prominent since the 1950s.

In this chapter I shall look at just a few illustrations which depict an expanding trend in British political and social life. The difference between political and social action is not always easy to perceive. A street demonstration, or mass protest, that begins as an orderly political event can become a civil riot. On the other hand, episodes that are basically civil riots can have unstated, implicit, political motivation. The demonstration against the invasion of Suez in 1956, described in Chapter 1 of this book, is an example of the former. The latter will be discussed in relation to the riots of the 1980s.

1. The Sixties' Time Bomb

The most regular confrontation between demonstrators and police in the early 1960s concerned nuclear weapons. CND (Campaign for Nuclear Disarmament) had started its Easter marches from the Aldermaston weapons testing centre to central London in the previous decade, and almost invariably a degree of physical conflict marked the London end of the march, but in retrospect, looking back, they were generally relatively limited skirmishes. By the middle of the decade, when CND energy began to run down a little, political episodes such as the white Rhodesian Unilateral Declaration of Independence caused restricted confrontations between protesters and police, but again they were not, on the whole, characterised by the viciousness of later incidents.

A new momentum began to be revealed in 1968, a year of great unrest virtually throughout the whole of Europe. At a time when universities across Britain were in turmoil, with students contesting the attitudes and decisions of the people who ran the institutions – the running of the London School of Economics, for example, was for a long time brought to a halt by an occupation by students, an example of 'The "instituted" against the "instituting"',[1] to use an important concept of the time. A series of demonstrations against the Vietnam War were organised in London. All ultimately centred on the USA's embassy in Grosvenor Square.

The tone was set in March 1968 when over 200 arrests were made at an anti-Vietnam War demonstration in which several thousands of people fought with police outside the embassy. Four months later, in July, an even larger crowd was confronted by a force of over a thousand police. On that occasion it was reported that about one thousand of the demonstrators broke away from the main crowd, smashing windows, damaging cars, ripping up paving slabs, starting fires and fighting running battles with the police. It was more serious than any previous disturbance, with the police unexpectedly losing control of a running crowd.

By October another demonstration was planned, and the representatives of law and order were more thoroughly prepared. On the morning of the protest even the non-sensational Sunday newspapers of 27 October 1968, such as the *Observer* and *Sunday Times*, reported that the police were prepared to use a force of around 14,000, and that London was barricaded for the day. There was general concern at the militancy expressed by the protest organisers, another relatively new development in the field of political demonstrations. Although nominally, or superficially, organised around a specific concern, the Vietnam War, unlike the earlier nuclear weapons and Rhodesia protests, this new development had wider purposes. Revolt against everything seemed to be on the agenda, and phrases such as guerrilla warfare were used, suggesting more serious action than a skirmish or two with a few policemen.

Callaghan, who was Home Secretary at the time, and therefore had ultimate responsibility for the policing of the event, later wrote of the demonstration: 'its organisers were busy during the summer, their advance publicity claiming that the "autumn offensive" was to be a massive affair. The *London Evening News* and *The Times* published accounts of what they called "startling plots" to use home-made bombs and of plans to seize sensitive installations and government buildings ... an agitated atmosphere built up ... with newspaper reports making the ordinary citizen's blood curdle about the horrors to expect.'[2] Though the fears were mostly overstated, reports of actual events did speak of banner stakes being hurled at police like spears, and of scaffolding, planks, bricks and fireworks being utilised as weapons. The liberal-tending *Guardian* of 28 October 1968 was as concerned as less tolerant newspapers about the violence.

It is impossible to say exactly when a collective mood changes, but it might be reasonable to suppose that 1968 did witness a change towards more mass street violence. Whether this is blamed mainly on the demonstrators or the police depends on your point of view. Right-wing commentators, and most of those in the mass media, largely blame the former; politically left-wing observers mainly cite police tactics and attitudes as causing it. Certainly some of the trade union disputes that involved the police during the following decade followed a similar pattern. The miners' strikes and the 1976–7 strike of Grunwick workers for union recognition, for instance, all experienced picket-line violence between strikers and police. That, however, was mild in comparison with the rioting that emerged in the 1980s.

2.   Thatcher's Black and White Riots: 1980–1

It was in the Thatcher regime that a different, and more profoundly disturbing, direction emerged in street politics. Once again the complete picture is extremely complex and I will attempt to illustrate it by discussing events of 1981 and 1985 in particular, but will begin with a short reference to 1980.

In April 1980, in the St Paul's district of Bristol, a police raid on suspected illegal drug dealers ended in a prolonged street riot. Reports spoke of youths, mostly of black youths, setting up no-go areas, in which they roamed freely without any police presence. Martin Kettle and Lucy

Hodges subsequently described why the police withdrew for a period: 'Of the 50 to 60 officers on the scene, 22 had been injured and had to be taken to hospital (27 more had minor injuries), 21 police cars were severely damaged and six were destroyed beyond repair . . . it is estimated that the police faced a crowd of 2000.'[3] This was written some months after the events, not in the heat of the moment, as mass-media reports are, and the authors had no reason to exaggerate descriptions and facts that had by then been clearly established. Kettle and Hodges claim that the rioters, although predominantly black, were not entirely so – a subtlety many of the news reporters missed. The social analysts Harris Joshua and Tina Wallace concluded that the episode was 'Indicative of the inability of the police to contain the kinds of social forces recently unleashed'.[4] It was essentially a previously unknown kind of riot, basically racial but with many other overtones, an extremely violent and destructive expression of hatred, frustration and despair for which the police were totally unprepared, and which deeply shocked British society in general.

Twelve months later a number of people died in a fire in the Deptford district of south-east London and a mass protest occurred at police handling of the investigation:

BATTLE AS BLACKS GO ON MARCH

a demonstration by 5,000 blacks erupted in violence

(Paul Brown, *Sun*, 3 March 1981)

Those two incidents might have been treated as alarm signals, but on the whole were dismissed by the authorities as merely isolated episodes. However, in the following month a very much greater catastrophe erupted in the south London area of Brixton.

On this occasion several pages of the country's most widely read newspaper were given up to the events. Over a front-page photograph of devastation it ran the headline: 'BATTLEFRONT' (James Lawthwaite, *Sun*, 13 April 1981). The idea of actual warfare was continued in the paper's leader column: '*The whole nation was appalled by the scenes of mindless violence and looting at Brixton.* Not since the Blitz has London seen such devastation . . . nearly 200 people were injured including 165 policemen' (ibid.). The direct link between the destruction caused by the rioting and the German aerial bombing of forty years earlier clearly indicated the alarm this outbreak created. The connection was pushed further on another page in a quotation from a policeman involved at the front line: 'THIS PLACE IS AT WAR' (James Wardlaw and Martin Turner, ibid.). There was no doubting the seriousness of the situation, and less than three months later there were outbreaks of rioting in other parts of the country.

The situation was obviously so critical that even the *Sun*, a newspaper that usually presented political affairs very simplistically, recognised something was happening beneath the surface of events. At the time of the earlier Brixton riots it had acknowledged in a small way a valid voice of dissent, referring to a black youth who 'blamed the police for all the trouble', and quoting him as saying 'There are too many of them here' (James Wardlaw and Martin Turner, *Sun*, 13 April 1981). Although almost uncritically Conservative, the paper was sufficiently stunned to admit there were reasons behind the actions: 'The Government must make bigger efforts to tackle the underlying causes of discontent in many urban areas – bad housing, deprivation, lack of jobs' (ibid.). This links with the later description of living conditions in Liverpool's Toxteth district: 'A depressing cocktail of slum housing, police harassment and too many people chasing too few jobs' (Colin Myler, *Sun*, 7 July 1981). This is important in presenting the police not only as victims of the violence, but also as a partial cause of it. It reflects a deep concern running through society as a whole that something was profoundly wrong.

Even so, a few days later the newspaper reverted to its sensational style to report a new outbreak of civil disorder:

BRIXTON EXPLODES AGAIN!

400 rioters fought a fierce hand-to-hand battle with police.

(George Hollingbery, *Sun*, 11 July 1981)

Despite the militaristic language the factual basis was confirmed by a more serious, and liberal-minded, newspaper. The *Guardian* (16 July 1981) reported a car being set alight, and crowds of young men in the streets wielding staves in a collective fury. The leading article of the previous day had commented on the features common to the virtually simultaneous riots in two areas of the capital, and the northern cities of Manchester and Liverpool, which were judged to be widespread destruction and physical viciousness.

At a governmental level the April riots in Brixton had prompted the setting up of an official inquiry, under the chairmanship of Lord Scarman. The inquiry was being carried out, of course, during the subsequent July conflict. Looking at the factors identified in newspapers (as quoted above) as possible causes of the riots, Scarman concluded: 'None of these features can perhaps usefully be described as a *cause* of the disorders. ... But taken together, they provide a set of social *conditions* which create a predisposition towards violent protest. Where deprivation and frustration exist on the scale to be found among the young black people of Brixton, the probability of disorder must, therefore, be strong.'[5] The police were severely criticised in the Report: 'The violence erupted from the spontaneous reaction of the crowds to what they believed to be police harassment. ... The riots were essentially an outburst of anger and resentment by young black people against the police'; although Scarman stressed that not all the rioters were black, the Report did conclude that 'There was a strong racial element in the disorders ... [though] they were not a race riot.'[6] The Report made wide-ranging recommendations, particularly regarding the problems of maintaining law and order, on the basis that: 'There is scope for a more coherent and better directed response by the police to the challenge of policing modern, multi-racial society.'[7]

By November 1981, when the Report was published, the situation had cooled down. As a consequence, the government felt it had done its job in commissioning the inquiry, and a few minor adjustments to policing were all that was needed. The issues of social conditions and any racial elements behind the violence were forgotten. That is, until September 1985.

3. Thatcher's Black and White Riots: 1985

After four years of relative quiet – though, of course, small incidents were continually occurring without making the front pages – tensions in the Handsworth area of Birmingham erupted in September 1985. In some ways the pattern appeared to be similar to that established earlier. Accounts of such confusing episodes often vary, but it was generally agreed there were two deaths, and in six hours of rioting fire bombs were used and firefighters pelted with petrol bombs. Cars were overturned and set alight to create barricades, arson was committed against factories and forty-five shops were destroyed. There was a similarity with the 1980–1 disorder in that the police and fire brigade had no control over the situation, the rioters commanded the streets.

In any event, general interest in that complication was quickly overcome by two horrendous events and outbreaks of mass violence during the following three weeks. The first occurred at the end of September when police in south London shot a black woman in a tragic, and in retrospect inexplicable, error. Brixton again erupted, with the burning of cars and buildings and a great deal of looting, at a cost estimated at the time to be £3 million. Again there were running fights between police and youths mostly described as black. An account published a week later gave the toll as: '99 cars were burnt, 83 shops were looted, two women were raped and 220 people arrested' (*The Economist*, 5 October 1985). Although the shooting of an innocent woman triggered the violence, the speed and ferocity with which it escalated suggest there were deep underlying causes that had been building up for some time. Joshua and Wallace's conclusion about the St Paul's riot in Bristol appeared to have been vindicated, justified, 'In the absence of serious political initiatives ... Future confrontations ... will be more violent.'[8]

Clearly any idea that co-operation, or even peaceful co-existence, between black youth and police had been created was an illusion. It was obvious, too, that such factors as very high unemployment and poor housing conditions remained, and perhaps had intensified, grown worse, during the period. There was a strong racial element in the new rioting, but that was not the entire problem. The Conservative-supporting *Daily Mail* reported that in Brixton: 'Thirty per cent of an estimated 1,500 rioters were white as were almost half the 220 people arrested' (Anthony Doran, 1 October 1985).

It was not a purely local issue either. As news of it flashed across the nation riots in other areas broke out: 'Stone-throwing youths confronted the police in full riot gear last night in Toxteth, Liverpool. Hijacked cars were turned into blazing barricades, firemen were stoned ... a police station was under siege' (*Daily Mail*, 2 October 1985). The embryo of frustration, despair, resentment among a generation – white as well as black – lost to what Conservatives referred to as the Thatcher economic miracle, obviously lived on.

Concerning itself with the complacent illusion of peace and cooperation, a weekly journal, whose writers had more time for thought than daily reporters, commented: 'Brixton police claim good relations with the black community and they do indeed have good relations with the mostly middle-aged and middle-class blacks who sit on their consultative committee. But the middle-aged and middle-class are not the problem. The young have no respect for the people the police want to treat as their leaders' (*The Economist*, 5 October 1985). This is perceptive observation from a journal that is by no means politically radical, and whose main concern is the interest of stable capitalism. Its worry was that generation and class were vital factors being left out of other analyses, and that economic stability could come only from a notion of perceived and accepted broad social fairness.

Once more events overtook thought, or sober reflection. Another black woman, this time in the north London area of Tottenham, died of a heart attack while police were searching her home after having arrested her son. News and rumour quickly exploded into extreme violence across the large, multi-racial Broadwater Farm estate. There were 243 casualties, including the shocking murder of a policeman who was attempting to defend firemen from attack. A weekly journal observed that a new dimension to urban rioting had emerged: 'The violence was more serious. ... A shotgun and a pistol were fired at the police, for the first time in rioting in mainland Britain' (*The Economist*, 12 October 1985). Again, apparently inexplicable police action, including a failure to believe that the woman concerned was actually dying, triggered the violence.

The *Daily Telegraph* as a newspaper that almost uncritically supports the Conservative government, and its ideas of law and order, admitted (8 October 1985) there was a linking thread between the disturbances, partly related to the nature of the policing carried out, and partly because the districts of Birmingham and London concerned are similar areas of deprivation. A resident was quoted, in the same edition of the paper, as expressing the opinion that the trouble was just waiting to happen, that the particular trigger was less important than the build-up of the atmosphere following the Handsworth explosion of fury and frustration.

The Economist too saw a link, but a more specific one: 'there is one certain connection between the riots in Handsworth, Brixton and Tottenham. It is the link which blacks see between incidents of police violence. ... They regard the police as agents of oppression' (12 October 1985). This indicates that rioting is not merely a response to local acts of what are perceived as police aggression, but that such actions are seen as more generally anti-black, although reports quoted above suggest that it was not only black youth that saw the police 'as agents of oppression'. The chief executive of the local authority, Harringay Council, was reported as saying, 'the youngsters ... were determined they were going to have some revenge' (David Whitfield, *Morning Star*, 8 October 1985). The word 'revenge' does suggest, whatever their colour, extremely strong feelings amongst 'the youngsters'. Unsurprisingly perhaps, *The Economist* saw the solution in economic terms: 'The root of the urban problem is, too evidently, idleness. ... Black people with jobs do not riot in the streets' (ibid.). Ignoring the white aspects of discontent, and treating the events as race riots, the same article proposed 'positive discrimination in favour of black people in education and jobs' as a solution. Positive discrimination, of course, is always open to the counter-argument that it might create other problems, perhaps of deprived white – or brown – resentment, and therefore backlash.

A number of the issues that re-emerged for urgent public debate had, in fact, been anticipated by analysts, but ignored by those in power. The academic John Benyon, for instance, had written in 1984, the previous year, 'Britain has a choice. Either we can take vigorous action to cure the problems which the riots and Lord Scarman's Report exposed or we can procrastinate and tinker, hoping that somehow the problems will go away, but more likely creating ghettos, characterised by deprivation and neglect, tough policing and disintegrating political authority.'[9] In the same book Scarman himself observed: 'There are still no signs of "an effective co-ordinated approach to tackling inner city problems".'[10] The events of the autumn of 1985 should not, in this light, have taken anyone by surprise.

In the wake of those incidents many commentators did realise that not all of the Scarman Report recommendations of four years earlier had been put into operation. Another formal inquiry was set up under Lord Gifford, which published its Report in July 1986. It was similar to Scarman's Report on Brixton in 1981. In his Introduction to the repub-lished edition of his Report Gifford quoted Scarman's own response to the 1986 document: 'It is saying very much the same as the Brixton report five years ago. Many of its proposals are no more than a repeat of the proposals you will find in the Brixton report.'[11] Once the publicity around the violence and destruction had died down very little was actually done. Some people found it ironic that following immediately after her third, record making, consecutive general election victory it was reported that: 'A TRIUMPHANT Margaret Thatcher is moving swiftly to take up a new challenge – beating the crisis in Britain's cities' (Gordon Greig, *Daily Mail*, 13 June 1987). The sceptics asked whose policies had created 'the crisis', and why it had taken so many years, and so much destruction, to recognise the 'new challenge'. Whether or not the crisis has actually been overcome only the future, rather than history, can tell.

4.   The Death of the Poll Tax

The Poll Tax, as it was commonly known, was introduced in Scotland in 1989, England and Wales in 1990. It replaced the former system of local taxation based on property, and although officially termed the Community Charge its common name came from the Old English word 'poll' meaning head, because it was a local, or council, tax on heads, or individuals, rather than property. Its financial unfairness caused widespread protests in Scotland, but they were little reported in the rest of Britain. It was not until the eve of its introduction in England and Wales, and a general realisation of the high levels of payment involved, that a powerful, and concerted, protest occurred against the tax Alan Watkins later called a 'brutally, simple notion'.[12]

A national demonstration had been planned to take place in London on the day before – which was conveniently a Saturday – the poll tax officially began. It started as a peaceful demonstration, but ended with reports of 341 people having been arrested, and 417 injured, including 331 police officers. There were the, by now, usual incidents of cars burning and a good deal of looting from shops. There was conflicting evidence of unprovoked police brutality and of vicious, intimidating demonstrators. Looking back, Waddington wrote: 'television news bulletins showed horrendous scenes of violence, including the apparently joyous destruction of shop windows; civilian cars being vandalised and set ablaze; demonstrators jumping for their lives from the paths of speeding police vans; a female protester being pathetically rolled along under the hooves of galloping police horses; police cars with scaffold staves driven through their side windows. ... During a day of incredible chaos, 1,985 separate crimes were reported, 408 people were arrested and three million pounds' worth of damage caused to property.'[13] In any kind of prolonged running urban battle different things are happening at different times and in different places. Where the emphasis is put depends on your political viewpoint. It is easy to isolate incidents and claim them as the whole picture, so that either the demonstrators or the police are complete villains, and therefore the other group are entirely blameless victims. Evidence provides only partial facts, and historical facts themselves need to be interpreted. You will notice here, for example, that the number of arrests increases in retrospect, which is not to say that either figure is wrong – but rather that they were calculated at different times, or perhaps in different ways.

To serious analysts it was clear that although the poll tax was the nominal issue, there were other very serious underlying tensions. Commenting on the idea that the most vigorous protesters were 'the young, the unemployed, the homeless', Waddington concludes: 'In terms of the political/ideological level of analysis, here was a powerless and disaffected section of society, aware that no-one within the present political system ...

was speaking on its behalf.'[14] The whole economic state of the nation, Thatcher's style of government and the desire on the part of some police and some demonstrators to confront one another, were all factors in the escalation of a peaceful protest into a full-scale riot. The leader column in the *Independent* for that Monday (2 April 1990) recognised more was at issue than a system of taxation, arguing in essence that the nature of civilisation itself, as a social form of organisation, was being questioned. One aspect of a civilised, civil, society is basically concerned with ways of organising the relationship between governors and governed, power to make decisions, and responsibility for carrying them out. That has become a recurrent crisis in Britain.

Immediately after the riot Thatcher expressed – in a television interview on 1 April 1990 – 'absolute horror' at the violence, although she refused to reconsider the policy of taxation. The poll tax, or community charge, lasted only three years, Thatcher herself remained prime minister for less than eight months longer. Neither the peaceful demonstration, nor the subsequent riot, directly caused either demise. The poll tax was closely identified with Thatcher's personal policy, and proved extremely unpopular in Tory areas once those people saw it in action. The riot, however, certainly drew attention to the tax, and opened up, in discussion of the riot itself, the whole political and financial debate about the issue in a way that had not been achieved by more intellectual argument.

Fighting in the streets is a very blunt form of political argument, and not to be supported or condoned in a constitutional civil society. Yet it has increasingly become a weapon in the second half of the twentieth century. There are many, and complex, causes of it, but in a sense violence is the ultimate form of communication. Its increase suggests a profound breakdown in the civil contract between decision-makers and the mass of people.

Chapter 5 Battles for Minds

It is obviously not as easy to measure attitudes and beliefs as it is to count votes, or produce statistics on economic performances or even estimates on how much damage has been done in financial terms by various forms of physical devastation. Yet attitudes and beliefs lie behind those other, more measurable, tangible factors, and some of the deepest changes in British society in the last four decades of the twentieth century have been in the minds of its citizens. In this chapter I shall look mainly at the broad area of equal opportunities, in particular those concerning ethnic minorities – which involves the issue of race relations – and women.

This does not mean other facets are of no interest, but is simply due to the demands of space. The theoretical concept of equal opportunities can cover a wide area, as indicated by the kind of job advertisement, now completely common, placed by local authorities: 'The Council as an Equal Opportunity Employer welcomes applications regardless of race, colour, nationality, ethnic origin, sex, marital status, disability or age' (*Opportunities*, 12 February 1993). Sometimes the idea of equal opportunities becomes mixed up with that of positive discrimination, of deliberate discrimination in favour of someone with characteristics that have been pre-determined on an ideological, or needs, basis. In cases of competition, for instance in a job vacancy, this entails discriminating in favour of someone who has a particular gender, colour, race, etc. – and therefore may entail possible discrimination against someone else of a different gender, colour, race, etc., which leads to the paradox of inequality being exercised in the name of equality. But then, politics and history are full of paradox.

One interesting aspect of social change during the period covered by this book, although there is not room to pursue it in detail, is changing general public attitudes to facets of sexuality. Divorce, abortion, extra-marital sexual activity, children born outside marriage, are all areas in which attitudes, and therefore behaviour, changed enormously from the 1960s. The changes can be very briefly illustrated with regard to intra-sexual experiences. It was not until 1967, for example, that homosexual acts between consenting adults in private became legal, and to have that sexual preference, or predilection, still usually meant a degree of public shame. By the 1990s there was no need for secrecy, and public figures were free to express their sexual preferences without meeting either official or unofficial significant displeasure. Sports personalities, and popular entertainers, suffered no decline in public admiration for open expression of what formerly would have been considered unacceptable sexual predilections. The actor Ian McKellan, for example, publicly forthright in his homosexuality, was knighted in 1991. That would have been, however wrongly, inconceivably shocking less than thirty years earlier. It is significant that the tabloid press eventually accepted the word gay as a universal description, as opposed to the earlier terms of queer or homo. The AIDS crisis that developed in the 1980s created some setback to the pace of liberation, or liberalisation, of attitudes, but not to an irrevocable, unchangeable, extent. Acceptance of overt behaviour common in the 1990s would have been unthinkable to the vast majority of people in 1960.

1. 'Genuine grievances and unreal fears'

After the Second World War there was considerable immigration into Britain from some of the Commonwealth countries, particularly the Caribbean and other 'coloured' nations. By 1960 the government was considering legal limitations on entry into Britain, and in 1962 the first Commonwealth Immigrants Act was passed by Parliament. That was followed during the decade by another Commonwealth Immigrants Act, two Race Relations Acts and the creation of the Race Relations Board. This represented a great deal of parliamentary activity on a very new issue. Immigration had been going on for a long time, but not in the same way as an issue for political concern – the political activist and journalist Keith Tompson has written of the 1962 Act: 'Race now took its place at the centre of national political life.'[1]

In the 1951 census there had been, for example, about 17,000 West Indians recorded as living in Britain, a year before the first Immigration Act this figure had risen ten-fold to about 173,000, and was continuing to increase. The official reason for limitation was fear of growing unemployment amongst the immigrant population, and the first Act restricted entry to people with a guaranteed job, or particular work skills. Unofficially, politicians were, at least to some extent, motivated by fear of racial violence breaking out as the immigrant population increased. These two factors continued to dominate the debate through the decade, with the argument about unemployment becoming supplemented by official concern about such aspects of the social infrastructure as housing, education and welfare services.

There was a great deal of political fudging of the issues, which suggests that however genuine the concerns about employment, housing and welfare services the fundamental motivation of the politicians was fear. The ambiguous and equivocal attitudes were observed at the time by an astute leader-writer commenting on the official pamphlet *Admission of Commonwealth Citizens to the United Kingdom*. That document had been produced with the stated purpose of helping people understand Britain's first Immigration Act, but *The Times* of 28 April 1962 criticised it for being bewildering, confusing rather than clarifying both the procedures and the issues. The newspaper commented on the fact that the crucial matter of colour was not mentioned, nor any reasons given for the new legislation. The official pamphlet appeared to deliberately avoid all the real questions. The source of this criticism is significant, it is not based on predictable leftish responses, but comes from within the establishment itself.

The 1964 general election campaign confirmed that race had become a central feature of British political, and social, life. The prime minister, Sir Alec Douglas-Home, himself made a speech which brought immigration into the election debate. Speaking in Bradford, one of the areas in which immigrants had begun to congregate, on 6 October 1964, and again two days later in Birmingham, Douglas-Home justified the Immigration Act on the grounds that it had been necessary, because without it a million immigrants would have flooded into Britain, creating economic problems of employment, housing and education. Statistics can always be, and usually are, argued about. In this case a million is speculation anyway. It helps to carry the idea of a flood of people, which is an emotive image, having all the associations of a destructive, out of control, catastrophe. Despite the rationalising aspects of employment, housing and education, a flood is something to be feared because it will destroy everything in its path.

The fear factor was certainly manipulated by a few politicians and elements of the mass media, yet in some areas of high immigration – and it has to be observed that in this context 'immigration', or 'Commonwealth immigrants', are euphemisms for the activities of black/brown people – the basis of fear did exist. Whether this sprang from sheer prejudice or not is another, and more sociological, question.

In the Perry Barr constituency district of Birmingham, in the industrial Midlands, race was a subdued, but definite, issue. A report in *The Times* (10 October 1964) featuring marginal seats focused in part on a young mother whose son was one of a white minority in his school class, who was worried about the increasing non-white population of the area, and blamed Labour Party attitudes for the problems caused by immigration. Journalists sometimes take the view of one person and present it as a widespread attitude, and therefore references to individuals have to be treated carefully. In this case, however, the single voice was evidently not alone. A Labour majority of 183 votes in 1959 became a Conservative victory by 327 in 1964. That is a tiny change, but it becomes more significant when we consider that in the country as a whole, the Conservatives lost a 100-seat parliamentary majority, with Labour becoming the government party for the first time since 1951. Race had undoubtably become a factor, and was a complex one.

This was especially illustrated by the more vicious campaign in Smethwick, another area of Birmingham. There a previous Labour majority of about 3,500 was turned into a Conservative victory of almost 2,000. Racism was an overt, though complex, electioneering issue. One of the slogans of the campaign was 'If you want a nigger neighbour vote Liberal or Labour', or variations on that theme. There was also, however, the personalities of the candidates to consider in this case. In an academic analysis, A. W. Singham concluded: 'In many ways Mr Gordon Walker was a sitting target. ... To many critics he appeared both distant and donnish ... he had never managed to establish that sense of identification with the voters at large which is so essential to a politician.'[2] In a thoughtful article written immediately after the election Dennis Barker (*Guardian*, 17 October 1964) warned against leaping to the obvious conclusion that it was entirely a racist result. Although conceding that racism was an important element, he also felt that the Labour victor in 1959 had lost touch with his constituents' concerns, pointing out that Gordon Walker had been Labour's shadow Foreign Secretary, whereas his opponent was involved in local politics. Voters, Barker argued, had complaints that were valid, and also fears that were not valid. The Labour candidate had failed to distinguish between these factors, and therefore to tackle them. Governments at the time, and since, failed to address that duality of justified grievances and unjustified fears.

Laws dealt with controlling the numbers of new immigrants, and attempting, as in the Race Relations Acts, to legislate the relationships between individual immigrants and the society into which they had come.

In retrospect the political theorist Shamit Saggar sees Walker's defeat as having longer-term consequences: 'The experience of losing the Shadow Foreign Secretary at the hands of the Smethwick electorate in 1964 meant that, from its earliest days, the Labour administration felt vulnerable and defensive on the immigration issue. ... The message that the electorate had little sympathy for would-be immigrants was first delivered at Smethwick.'[3] For Saggar this helps to explain the apparent paradox that the Labour governments of 1964–70 appeared to follow basically Tory policies on immigration, although with modifications. In the struggle over attitudes, the battle for minds, there were voices recommending tolerance and understanding, but they tended to be drowned by those of prejudice.

2. 'Rivers of blood'?

External events forced something of a crisis when, in the autumn of 1967, a few years after gaining independence, the nationalist government of the east African state of Kenya began expelling its citizens of Asian origin. It was estimated that 170,000 people were entitled to enter Britain under the existing laws, and that approximately half of that number had applied for passports by October 1967. As the issue grew over the following months even some liberally inclined commentators began to accept the idea of control. The *Observer* (18 February 1968), for instance, reported without comment that a new peak of a thousand Kenyan Asians a week coming into Britain had been reached, and that the Government was contemplating restricting the inflow to around 6,000 a year. Those people generally went to live in areas in which there were already immigrant populations, of course, so that the density in some regions was increased whilst other localities were entirely unaffected.

The Conservative MP Enoch Powell, who represented a Midlands constituency that was affected, had become the centre of the racial controversy. In April 1968, speaking in the west Midlands, he said: 'Britons in some areas had been made strangers in their own country by the inflow of immigrants. ... In 15 or 20 years, on present trends, there will be in this country 3,500,000 Commonwealth immigrants and their descendants. ... As I look ahead, I am filled with foreboding. Like the Roman, I seem to see "the River Tiber foaming with much blood".'[4] The speech caused a national uproar. Powell had been a Professor of Classics and was making a textual quotation in what became the most notorious phrase in the speech, but that did not lessen its impact, and in any case it was immediately taken out of context and re-phrased as 'rivers of blood'.[5] Powell was immediately dismissed from the shadow cabinet by Heath, and the former's views officially repudiated, but he retained supporters within the Conservative Party.

It is one of the paradoxes of politics and history that, within days, a previously virulently anti-Tory group of workers expressed support for Powell. The workers of London docks – such people and such a working place existed in 1968 – called a spontaneous strike and marched to the House of Commons to voice their approval of Powell. This caused a great deal of embarrassment and bewilderment to many radicals and liberals. The *Observer* of 28 April 1968, for example, expressed a sense of disbelief that such action could have happened, attributing it to working-class fear about the effects of immigration on housing, education and employment. Despite this revelation, it might be argued that governments of both parties continued to address the symptoms of racial disharmony, rather than its base causes.

The *Observer* sent two reporters, one Indian the other English, to Powell's constituency for a month. Dilip Hiro regretfully reported that he was saddened to have discovered that the liberal idea that children receiving a racially mixed education will grow up as tolerant adults was not borne out by his experiences in Wolverhampton. In the same edition of the paper (14 July 1968) the leader-writer noted that Britain was caught in a dualism: facing the possibility of profoundly disruptive racial conflict; or of being the first nation to achieve full racial, multi-cultural, harmony. There is no doubting the tension that existed at the time. It was in this context and atmosphere of delicate, and uncertain, equilibrium that the Labour government passed the second Commonwealth Immigrants, and Race Relations, Acts.

In this vortex of intolerance the Race Relations Act of 1968 was a genuine attempt, whether or not it succeeded, to legislate equality in behaviour. It attempted to define illegal behaviour as treating one person less favourably than another on the basis of their race, colour, ethnic or national origins. In theory, making intolerant behaviour unlawful would eventually lead to attitudes of tolerance in the majority, and avoid resentment building up amongst the minorities. Once the minds of all people had been won over to harmony there could be no threat of 'rivers of blood'.

3. Another 'Flood'

Immigration continued, disputes over it recurred, and intolerant behaviour and attitudes were not stopped, or eradicated, though fear of mass violence calmed down. The next major crisis was again created, or precipitated, by external events, and again in east Africa. General Idi Amin, the dictator of Uganda, expelled Asians from the country in 1972. The idea of the arrival of tens of thousands of additional immigrants caused mixed responses. Predictably, Powell raised the fear factor: 'hundreds of thousands of our fellow citizens here in Britain are living in perpetual dread ... for themselves ... for the future, or they dread for both. There are those ... who live in actual physical fear ... as if they are trapped or tied to a stake in the face of an advancing tide' (speech given at Ramsgate, 12 September 1972). Even the vocabulary had not changed much, but by 1972 the impact was greatly reduced.

There were objections, but in muted forms. Even those elements in the national press that had been in favour of tighter controls on immigration were moderate, or even supportive of the potential immigrants. Practical difficulties arose, as the *Daily Telegraph* (31 August 1972), in particular, reported, for instance: the New Towns Commission complained that there would not be room for any more Ugandan Asians in the new towns. The following day the same newspaper recorded that a number of Midlands' cities had come to a similar conclusion. In contrast, the *Sun* 'welcomed' the first '193 men, women and children' to arrive, reporting 'official smiles ... kindness, tea and fruit cake', and quoting one of the new immigrants as saying 'we thank you for giving us this chance' (Peter Game and Michael Fielder, 19 September 1972). The conflicts of the 1960s may appear to have ended in harmony, but as later events were to show it was merely superficial.

I have dwelt at some length on the sixties in particular because most of the current problems of race, or ethnic origin, stem from that period. The street violence and disorders of the 1980s can be seen in part, though only in part, as race riots (cf. Chapter 4), and in so far as that is true, the majority of the rioters were probably born in that crucial era. A great many of the black people under the age of twenty rioting in 1985 were not themselves immigrants, but the children of immigrants, human products of a decade that failed to solve, or even fully face up to, what were unique problems. It is no longer possible, of course, to claim the problems are unique – but they will certainly be a feature of third millennium British society.

4. The Future?

The final decade of the second millennium began with just over two and a half million people in Britain belonging to officially defined ethnic-minority groups. That population is growing naturally: 'One in five of the White population is aged under 16 compared with one in three of the ethnic minority population as a whole ... those over 60 form a larger proportion of the White population (one in five) than they do in the ethnic minority populations (one in twenty).'[6] Another possible pointer to future development revealed the splits, or schisms, within the immigrant community as a whole when a widely reported manifesto, published in July 1990, demanded the formation of an official Council of British Muslims to function as a form of Muslim Parliament. Whether such an organisation could promote Muslim interests without causing alarm and resentment amongst other groups in society – including other ethnic minorities of course – remained a moot question.

Clearly race, racism and equal opportunities are complex matters. Whilst it can be said 'It is white racism that keeps ethnic minorities at the bottom of the hierarchy',[7] and a National Opinion Poll suggested, in July 1991, that racist views were not uncommon in Britain, there remain anomalies. For example, in 1983 at least 80 per cent of the ethnic minorities voting in the general election supported the Labour Party; in 1987, although statistics for the Afro-Caribbean population were similar, amongst Asians Labour support had dropped to below 70 per cent. The Opinion Poll referred to above indicated that 79 per cent of black people interviewed thought Britain racist, whilst only 56 per cent of Asians agreed. These figures suggest those with Asian ethnicity feel more comfortable in general than specifically black people.

In that Poll, two-thirds of white people felt Britain to be racist, and the fact that a majority appear to be aware of it perhaps implies, as the *Independent on Sunday* (7 July 1991) commented, that the situation will eventually change towards greater equality, because whites are becoming more conscious of non-white problems. In view of the statement in 1986 of the man who was to become head of the Commission for Racial Equality in 1993, this is perhaps a genuinely hopeful development. Herman Ouseley stated the need for white attitudes to change: 'Dismantling racism in cities is not a new priority for black people: it has been an issue for the decades that they have been there. Dismantling racism is now a priority for white people, because it is whites who have the control.'[8]

This hope has to be seen tentatively in the context of earlier attitudes still prevailing. The Conservative MP Winston Churchill, for instance, made what were generally considered to be Powellite remarks, in June 1993, suggesting that the issue of immigration was festering due to an unhealthy censorship. Another MP, Piara Khabia, challenged Major on the political status of Churchill's speech: 'Will the Prime Minister personally condemn the speech. ..? It has ... encouraged the fascists and racists to indulge in destructive activities.' Major replied guardedly: 'On the day it was published it did not represent my views' (*Hansard*, 8 June 1993). The winning of minds to tolerance and understanding is not an easy or quick matter, not something to be achieved in thirty or forty years, or with facile slogans.

5. Women's Liberation

There are obvious differences between race relations and gender relations, but even putting it in that way indicates similarities too. The main demands of the first national women's conference, as stated in the *Women's Newspaper* of 6 March 1971, were for: equal pay, education and opportunities; round-the-clock nurseries; unrestricted free contraception and abortion. The ideals of equality of pay, education and opportunity for all citizens became enshrined in the Commission for Equal Opportunities set up in 1975, and the Commission for Racial Equality created two years later. Both women and immigrants faced problems of prejudice and preconception that potentially led to various forms of deprivation. But legislation in itself does not necessarily lead to changes in perception and psychology: winning minds involves changing attitudes, and therefore behaviour.

In 1960, or even 1970, there were many avenues closed, or at least partly blocked, to women that had opened up by the nineties, though numerous areas in which women face irrational prejudices and difficulties remain. Demands conceded in law have not always been entirely translated into practice. In some cases the mind continues to be a bastion of resistance to new ideas.

Although some forms of a women's movement appeared at least as early as the eighteenth century, in contemporary terms the late 1960s, and especially the early seventies, were crucial times. Two seminal books were both published in 1970. The feminist literary theorist Mary Eagleton has written of one: 'It is difficult to overestimate the impact of Kate Millett's

Sexual Politics;[9] and the historian Arthur Marwick described the other, Germaine Greer's *The Female Eunuch*, as 'The critical event ... in the development of the contemporary feminist movement in Britain'.[10] There were, of course, other influential books, but Greer provided a rallying call in rejecting mere reformism: 'Revolution is the festival of the oppressed ... along our female road to freedom. ... The old process must be broken, not made anew.'[11] In essence it was a demand for argument supplemented by action, which was answered in various ways.

The psychoanalyst and feminist Juliet Mitchell has defined a central area of intellectual action:

> what is important is that feminism in initiating a system of thought, transforms the ideological notion that there is a biological opposition between the sexes which determines social life, and asserts instead that there is a contradiction in the social relations between men and women. This contradiction – which is never static, as a biological opposition would be – shifts, moves and is moved and is therefore one force among others that effects social change and the movement of human history itself.[12]

This has indeed become a major tenet in feminist theory, linking the rejection of the overriding importance of biology with demand for analysis of its use as a tool of social oppression.

Connecting the ideas of feminism and liberation, Mitchell and Ann Oakley have commented on the period of the early seventies: 'The "women's liberation movement" became the "women's movement". ... Women's liberationists took a sideways step closer to radical feminists and became "feminists".'[13] Perhaps one of the key aspects in that development, and a manifestation of action designed to change minds, attitudes and behaviour in society at large, was the 1970 conference: 'A recurrent theme at Britain's first Women's Liberation conference ... was "mystification". The pedestal is a put-down. Women might be "revered" but were lied to about their history, prospects and personality. Each individual woman's full development was murdered by a male-dominated society's exaggerated emphasis on her "biological role"' (*New Society*, 5 March 1970). Greer's revolution towards freedom for women, the argument ran, was to reject the patronage of a patriarchal society that was essentially oppressive, mystifying its own true nature, and that of women, in order to keep women subservient, and excluded from important areas of activity.

Twelve months later the first national women's liberation demonstration took place in London. The journalist Jill Tweedie commented in the *Guardian* (8 March 1971) that it was less an attempt to make new converts to the cause than to create a feeling of self-confidence amongst those already committed to it. Many embryonic movements need that aspect of solidarity. Further manifestations of confidence, and examples of public voices, were the creation of the magazine for feminist polemic *Spare Rib* in 1972, and the publisher Virago, set up with the express purpose of providing a discriminatory 'female-writers only' outlet, the following year. Both became successful commercial ventures within the field of capitalist publishing.

Although it was not an entirely satisfactory organisation from the point of view of the women's movement, the creation of the Commission for Equal Opportunities (CEO), in 1975, can be seen as a measure of the movement's success in the battle for minds. Whatever the Commission's inadequacies, its foundation was achieved within five years or so of equality of opportunity becoming a public issue, and that might be measured against the fact that racial discrimination had been in the public arena for almost twenty years before the Commission for Racial Equality (CRE) was set up in 1977. The Equal Pay Act and the Sex Discrimination Act were also created in 1975. The Commission's first head, Lady Howe, was reported as commenting, on the inauguration of CEO, that the work would be one of gradual enlightenment rather than overnight change. This sentiment clearly recognises that CEO is involved in a battle for minds, to change attitudes, and that it is part of a continuing process, not the end of a struggle.

The media in general reported enthusiastically that discrimination in advertising would be outlawed, and that advertisers were to be encouraged not to show women performing domestic duties in order to sell household products. Job advertisements were to become unisex, with such traditional terms as 'firemen' being replaced by 'firefighters'. There was also some interest in the Commission's desire to root out what it called 'sexist' children's books, which depicted boys in dominant roles.

A long tradition in which newspapers segregated job advertisements on gender lines came to an end, and jobs could not be advertised as being suitable for only male applicants. However, anyone who has seen British television advertisements for washing-up liquid or other domestic products will realise gender stereotyping has not entirely disappeared. The problem of education and language remains a central feminist concern. Arguing on the basis that language does not simply express ideas but actually helps to form them, such gender-exclusive terms of the past as chairman and spokesman have been criticised as endorsing a dominant patriarchal ideology. The terms chairperson and spokesperson have subsequently become the norm, although not without acrimony in the battle for minds.

A practical move towards diminishing traditional attitudes about the 'biological role' of women, and its limitations, was made in a provision that came into force in 1977 in the Employment Protection Act. This gave women the right to six weeks' paid maternity leave when they have a baby and, perhaps even more importantly, the opportunity of returning to their job, or a similar one, for up to 29 weeks after the birth of the baby. It had been argued, and continues to be, that women are discriminated against in careers because they break them in order to have children and bring them up. Maternity leave on its own certainly does not cover maybe twenty years of being a full-time mother of a family, and the consequent loss of status and experience when returning to work after such a long break; nor does it touch on the problem of twenty-four-hour nurseries. It has, however, allowed some women more flexibility in organising their lives.

6. Liberated Women?

A revolution cannot simply stop. It is not possible to halt processes with the attitude that life is now fine and we'll just keep things as they are. Process may continue as progress, change for the better, or it may reverse, not with a direct return to the old ways, but with a diversion that leads to reaction. When a revolution does appear to stop it usually quickly hardens into stagnation. In the 1990s, different attitudes to the position of women who have been liberated by the seventies' revolution emerged:

> The position of women is often considered to have improved during the last few decades. There is, however, considerable debate as to the extent of change ... some writers, pointing ... to the formal equality that women have with men, suggest that women are now fully emancipated, and have no need for any further changes. Others ... argue that women still have a long way to go before they are fully liberated.[14]

No serious journalist would now summarise the qualities of a woman as being an attractive girl of 25, as Linda Blandford was generally described in the media when she became the BBC's first on-camera female reporter in March 1968. There is more than a hint of patronage in that kind of language. In career terms there has been some perhaps unexpected female advance. The *Independent* (19 June 1993), for example, reported the qualification of Britain's first two women fighter pilots. Many more women have established themselves in such positions of power as company directors than there were in the 1960s. In terms of formal political power, in the 1964 general election the three main parties put forward 80 women candidates, 28 of whom were elected, which was the largest number up to that time. In the 1992 election there were over 300 female candidates, of whom 60 gained parliamentary seats. That was again the biggest ever number of women MPs. These simple statistical facts illustrate the difficulty of interpreting history and society. You might argue that in 1964 over a third of women candidates were successful, and that dropped to less than 20 per cent in 1992, indicating more prejudice against them. Also, across the period the number of female MPs increased by only 32, and the number in 1992 remained less than 10 per cent of the total membership of the House of Commons. On the other hand, the number of women candidates has increased four-fold, showing less prejudice against their selection, and the number of women MPs has more than doubled in less than thirty years. Interpretation of facts is influenced by perceptions of life as a whole.

As always there are ambiguities and paradoxes in the relationship of theory and practice. Feminism has consistently claimed to hold the politically radical ground, yet a female political biographer has written: 'by 1970 the Conservative Party depended on women not only as the majority of the electorate but also as the sex more faithful to Conservatism'.[15] Of course, those circumstances might have been changed by feminist activities.

In any event the struggle to change attitudes continues. In the University of Oxford a majority of academics (known as Dons) came into conflict, in May 1993, with the university's decision-making body over the promotion of women. The Dons proposed, by the overwhelming margin of 182 to 37 votes, to ask the university to accelerate the process of gender equality in the field of promotion. More than twenty years after the liberating revolution began, this kind of institutional conservatism persists, but a change in the thinking of individuals has occurred. It is extremely unlikely that in 1960, or 1970, a majority of Dons, mostly men, would have voted in the way they did. There is clearly a difference between the way in which individuals think and the inertia, the failure, or reluctance, to move on the part of an institution. It is something of a paradox in the circumstances that in the academic world women's studies courses, unknown in 1970, were the main growth area in higher education from the mid-seventies, existing in most higher education institutions by the 1990s, and had become an important factor in the re-education of social attitudes, and one of the successes of contemporary feminism.

The ambivalence felt by, and about, women's roles in society in the last decade of the century was perhaps summarised by the Princess of Wales. Speaking at an intensely reported conference on Women and Mental Health, on 1 June 1993, not long after her own marital problems and formal separation from the Prince of Wales, she said: 'If we, as a society, continue to disable women by encouraging them to believe they should only do things that are thought to benefit their family, even if these women are damaged in the process; if they feel they never have the right to do anything that is just for themselves; if they feel they must sacrifice everything for their loved ones, even at the cost of their health, their inner strength and their own self-worth, they will live only in the shadow of others and their mental health will surely suffer.' Although this does not utilise the polemical discourse theoretical feminism has established, it seemed to some observers a very eloquent articulation of the situation. The Princess of Wales believes there is still much to be achieved, but that does not preclude some achievement having been made.

7. Dissent and Backlash

In any struggle for hearts and minds there may be a point at which the intensity of the process creates schisms, or splits, among the participants, and the ferocity of the argument for tolerance may take it into what some people see as intolerance. There may also be differences of opinion on strategies for achieving specific aims. The feminist writer Rosalind Delmar has observed: 'Over the past twenty years a paradox has developed at the heart of the modern women's movement: on the one hand there is the generality of its categorical appeal to all women, as potential participants in a movement; on the other hand there is the exclusivism of its current internal practice, with its emphasis on difference and division.'[16] At the beginning of a journey there is not much doubt about the sense of direction, but the further along the road to freedom, to use Greer's metaphor, the movement goes the more possible paths open up, and the one goal of 'freedom' is fragmented into many potential aims.

The initial motivators of the seventies' revolution have been challenged on details – though not necessarily the fundamentals – of their thought. Professor Cora Kaplan, for instance, an influential feminist voice, has written of Millett's 'errors in her definition of patriarchy and the function of patriarchal ideology'.[17] Potentially the debate arising from this difference of interpretation is not simply concerned with an objective view of 'patriarchal ideology', but more with the position of initial perception. We all tend to see things from where we are ideologically standing ourselves. The kind of ideological concepts that have emerged in feminist polemics in the 1990s have been 'post-feminism', 'revisionism' and 'backlash', indicating the fragmentation that has arisen since the early days. That complexity may be seen as an inevitable aspect of development, and the academic Margaret Marshment has stated a nineties' view that perhaps does maintain a sense of direction: 'Representation is a political issue. Without the power to define our own interests and to participate in the decisions that affect us, women . . . will be subject to the definitions and decisions of others.'[18]

An aspect of the backlash element in the battle for minds comes from those people who feel the pleaders for tolerance may have gone too far in condemning the unconverted, that intolerance cannot entirely be fought by intolerance; and that positive discrimination, as it is known, is still discrimination. The Labour Party has an annual election amongst its MPs to choose the group which will lead the party in Parliament, a shadow cabinet. A new rule was introduced in 1993 compelling all Labour MPs to vote for at least four female candidates, the purpose of which was to have more women elected. In fact fewer women were elected than in the previous year. A number of journalists in the newspapers of 21 October 1993 revelled in the idea of a backlash against the attempt to create positive discrimination in favour of women, even writing of male revenge. The MPs' actions might be interpreted in at least two ways: that people who are forced by ideological pressures to accept positions of political correctness in public may, nevertheless, in private rebel against something they see as intolerant discrimination. Alternatively, the actions of those men can be seen as displaying such depth of anti-female interests that even stronger laws need to be applied against their prejudice. In the event, Smith appointed one of the women, Harriet Harman, who had been defeated, anyway – thereby imposing left-wing ideology over the democracy it had created.

The concept of political correctness – often abbreviated to PC – appears to the dissenters to impose a form of moral absolutism on social attitudes that is unacceptable. Indeed, the theatre critic John Peter has argued (*Sunday Times*, 10 January 1993) to the effect that, using the war zone of language, PC has developed neo-fascist tendencies. This refers back in part to the 1975 British legislation changing 'firemen' to 'fire-fighters', etc. But through the eighties and into the nineties that kind of linguistic thinking had extended to descriptive words that are sometimes used as terms of abuse, such as fat. Alternative commentators have pointed out the illogicality of many PC expressions. For example, to refer to someone as differently-sized implies a norm, and is therefore just as offensive as saying they are fat, but a good deal more patronising. The battle for minds may be one of persuasion rather than policing. The dilemma is that language can carry unconscious attitudes, therefore the problem becomes one of consciousness, of awareness, and ultimately slogans are too blunt an instrument to achieve that. Britain remains in a dynamic, and somewhat ambivalent, state in its attitudes and beliefs.

Chapter 6 'b ... y furriners'

When the Polish born, English language novelist Joseph Conrad referred to himself as a 'b ... y furriner'[1] he was satirising himself, his own pronunciation of English, censorship rules that frowned on the word 'bloody', and general British attitudes to foreigners. That was in 1898, at the height of the British Empire, when 'bloody foreigners' were considered a necessary nuisance in the world. Some people would argue that the same view existed in, and has continued since, 1960.

The Second World War, in reality, marked the end of the British Empire, although the dismantling process went on until the 1960s. Indeed, it may be argued that psychologically those processes are still going on – that some Britons cling to an emotional idea of empire, despite the falseness of such a position. The Conservatives' 1987 advertising campaign, quoted earlier in this book, repeated the message 'BRITAIN IS GREAT AGAIN'. The greatness was not specifically defined, but there was an implication of the nation being 'GREAT' again in the world. Certainly, one of Thatcher's repeatedly claimed achievements was in the field of international affairs and foreign policy.

From the late 1940s through to the 1960s many British colonies were granted, or won, independence. The word Empire was no longer used, having been replaced by the concept Commonwealth, a looser association of states who are free to join or leave, unlike a colony, which has no choice. Many of the newly independent countries, former colonies, did choose to join the Commonwealth of Nations. By 1960 the European Economic Community (EEC) had been formed by its original six members, with Britain outside it and unsure of its relationship to a political group that appeared to be led by the anti-British French president, Charles de Gaulle. The notion that Britain had lost an empire without having found a new role was a prevalent, not uncommon, one. It has been summarised by the political journalist Leslie Stone: 'For much of the 1960s, Britain suffered from an acute identity crisis, uncertain of its position and status in the world, unsure of its current power and future direction.'[2]

This chapter will mainly consider three broad areas of Britain's relationship with 'bloody foreigners' during and since the 1960s. They overlap to some extent, but for ease of reference I shall divide them into: (1) Britain as a solo power, in which the government of the day attempted to pursue a foreign policy independent of other nations; (2) the foreign policy adopted in conjunction with the United States of America and the United Nations; (3) the relationship with the European Community (EC)/European Union (EU) still popularly known as the Common Market, or as just simply, Europe; and (4) in conclusion I will touch on the Commonwealth.

1. Britain Goes It Alone

This section will concentrate on two issues: the Rhodesian Unilateral Declaration of Independence, that ran through the period from the mid-1960s to the end of the following decade; and the war in the Falkland Islands that dominated the early and mid-1980s, the issues from which remained unresolved into the following decade. Although they are not the only illustrations of Britain acting independently, both can be considered matters of immense importance.

The Southern Rhodesian Crisis

As a legacy, or inheritance, of empire in 1965 Britain had constitutional power over the country of Southern Rhodesia (now known as Zimbabwe) in the southern region of Africa. At that time the government in Southern Rhodesia, running the country's day-to-day affairs, was white-dominated, and feared the British Labour government would use its constitutional power to impose black majority rule on the colony. In November 1965 the Southern Rhodesian government's prime minister, Ian Smith, announced an illegal Unilateral Declaration of Independence (UDI), which in effect made the country entirely self-governing, a situation designed to maintain the political/racial *status quo*. A typical newspaper editorial condemned it as a 'rebellion without a shred of moral force. It is an act of wicked and suicidal folly' (*Sun*, 12 November 1965). The British prime minister, Harold Wilson, described the Southern Rhodesian government as being 'hell-bent on illegal and self-destroying action' (*Hansard*, 11 November 1965).

It was not merely a domestic dispute. The issue of black majority rule in African nations was one of international concern, and the prospect of a white minority perpetuating its domination was unacceptable to most of the world's governments. Britain immediately imposed economic sanctions on the rebel government – mostly in the form of banning trade with the country – partly in an attempt to conclude the rebellion, partly to forestall military intervention by other governments. British fears were expressed in the headline:

WILSON WILL URGE UN

'DO NOT USE FORCE'

(*Sun*, 12 November 1965)

The same edition of the paper explained: 'The Government's whole aim has been to play it calmly and not do anything that could provoke bloodshed.'

Speaking to Parliament, Wilson put the possibilities in emotive terms: 'We may have to face the prospect in Africa, which I don't find comforting, of the Red Army in blue berets. . . . Unless we show that our measures are likely to produce results' (*Hansard*, 12 November 1965). The 'measures' were economic sanctions, and the required 'results' a restoration of legal government in Southern Rhodesia with the consequent policy of moving towards majority black rule. The fear was that the USSR, 'the Red Army', would get a foothold in southern Africa as part of a United Nations invasion force, the 'blue berets'. Another newspaper editorial, usually hostile to Wilson, was in agreement with him on this issue. The *Daily Telegraph* of 13 November 1965 strongly rejected any claims of the United Nations to interfere, or intervene in the crisis, and provided Wilson with welcomed, and somewhat unexpected, support.

The alternative to economic sanctions or UN invasion was the use of military force by Britain alone. The situation created another historical and political paradox. The British right-wing, who were usually militaristic, were rather sympathetic to the white Rhodesians and therefore against using an invasion force on this occasion. Some of the left, however, normally anti-imperialist and many theoretically inclined towards pacifism, wanted military intervention to crush what they saw as a right-wing rebellion. Simultaneously the Rhodesians were announcing UDI and sending messages of loyalty to the Queen.

Although the *Sun* had praised Wilson's policy of avoiding 'bloodshed', there were less creditable, more purely political reasons for not invading.

The government did successfully resist international pressures to launch a military invasion of Southern Rhodesia, and in addition to feelings about having policy dictated by foreigners, one reason was uncertainty about how militarily effective such a mission might be, another was the possibility the action might split the Labour Party and inflict profound damage on it. The analyst Joseph Frankel has written: 'It seems clear that the occasion to use force in an action which was internationally demanded was abandoned owing to domestic pressures.'[3] This suggests that Wilson did not pursue a policy independent of international pressures simply for the sake of independence itself, but because he was cautious about creating friction amongst his own, divided, party members. That was a real problem. In 1968, for example, in a parliamentary vote on the situation in Southern Rhodesia, 51 Labour MPs wanting stronger action actually voted against the government, whilst others failed to support the prime minister, by abstaining.

Although the UN did not directly intervene, UDI continued to be an acute embarrassment to the British government. Wilson had two sets of negotiations with Smith, in 1966 on HMS *Tiger* and in 1968 on HMS *Fearless*. Neither the Tiger nor the Fearless talks, as they became known, led to a resolution, and to many observers it looked as though Wilson had been out-manoeuvred. Indeed, when Wilson lost power in the 1970 general election the rebel Southern Rhodesian government had existed comfortably for nearly five years. Succeeding governments had no more success.

The problem dragged on in all for fifteen years, and Morgan's analysis of its eventual conclusion gives no credit to any British government: 'Remarkably ... the seeds of change emerged in Rhodesia itself. Under pressure from the South African government, and in the face of growing guerrilla warfare, Ian Smith unexpectedly announced on 24 September 1976 that there would be majority rule in the country within two years.'[4] In 1979 Rhodesia/Zimbabwe's first black prime minister was elected, and the following year the constitutional crisis was finally and officially resolved: 'It was an astonishing climax to the long-running Rhodesian crisis. But it owed everything to political manoeuvres and economic pressures in southern Africa, and nothing to British influence.'[5] It was a salutary lesson for Britain, illustrating on one hand the country's inability to pursue an entirely solo foreign policy; on the other hand, it could be interpreted as an illustration that if a solo policy was to be effective it had to be applied with absolute confidence, rigour and immediacy, rather than as long-term economic sanctions. It is perhaps not a coincidence that the Rhodesian crisis was formally resolved at the beginning of Thatcher's first term in power, although outside her influence. It may be that she took that as a lesson against a soft approach to crises.

Britain Goes It Alone: The Falklands

The Falkland Islands are about four hundred miles from Argentina, and an interest in them was acquired by Britain (more accurately, England and Wales) as early as the sixteenth century. The islands were then considered to have strategic importance in the naval rivalry between England and Spain. The islands have been a British colony continuously since 1833, and inhabited by people of British stock. In 1967–8, during the time of the Southern Rhodesian crisis, there had been a diplomatic dispute between Britain and Argentina over the Falklands, but that had been covered over by a vague agreement referring final settlement to an unspecified future date.

In April 1982 the Argentine military dictatorship, perhaps in order to deflect interest from its own problems, invaded the Falkland Islands, claiming them as part of its own political and administrative territory. The British government assembled a military task force, and in an operation combining army, navy, air force and specialist units, re-took the islands just over two months later, in June. Two consequences were the strengthening of Thatcher's prime ministerial position in Britain, and the fall of the Argentinian government from power. The actual war was relatively short, yet the interest, concern and later controversy it caused were enormous.

'IT'S WAR!'

When Argentina occupied the Falkland Islands on Friday 2 April 1982 it took most British people very much by surprise. One Saturday morning newspaper expressed the immediate reaction of some people, that the Falklands could not be recovered by military means (*Guardian*, 3 April 1982). The tabloid paper the *Sun*, which played a controversially jingoistic role during the following weeks, nevertheless caught the mood of amazement of most people with its Saturday headline:

IT'S
WAR!

On this occasion the *Sun* was actually more accurate than the *Guardian*, which could not contemplate a military campaign. Parliament met in an emergency session and agreed, although with some MPs dissenting, with the government's intention to recover the islands, by force if necessary.

The extent of the shock caused by the situation, and the pace at which events seemed to happen, is measured in part by the immediacy of rumours regarding a possible plot within government administrative circles, and the speed at which they were countered by the administrators with claims of political incompetence on the part of their masters. The *Guardian*, and some other branches of the media, reported on 5 April 1982 that the Director-General of the Falkland Islands Office in London had accused the British Foreign Office of withholding information about Argentinian preparations for invasion. His accusation was in part based on the idea that it would have taken the invaders three weeks to bring the force together, and that activity could not have been undertaken in complete secrecy. The civil servants involved replied by blaming the government for not acting on the information it had been sent. Professor Lawrence Freedman has written that the subsequent official inquiry, the Franks Report, which cleared the government of charges of incompetence, 'was widely greeted with derision as something of a whitewash, and substantial evidence was found in the main body of the report to undermine [its] conclusion'.[6]

Official amazement was paralleled by that of ordinary people. The magnitude of events did not fully sink in immediately. In early April a survey of public opinion showed '39 per cent ... thought the Falklands was the most important issue facing the country, exactly the same percentage as chose unemployment'.[7] However, the passing of a month at war 'saw the Falklands as by far the most important [issue] (61 per cent) with unemployment now well behind (25 per cent)'.[8] Obviously, actual unemployment had not decreased dramatically in a single month, it was rather that the perceptions of the public about its relative importance had changed. The Falklands crisis was no longer a trivial dispute a long way off with a second-rate nation, it had become seen as a real war. A series of MORI opinion polls showed that people also became increasingly supportive of the government as decisive action was seen to be taken. In mid-April, 60 per cent of people were recorded as expressing satisfaction with the government's handling of the crisis, a week later that had risen to 68 per cent, but by the end of May, when British troops had actually landed on the Islands, it had risen to 84 per cent. This desire for strong action had opponents, of course, but support for the military task force the government quickly dispatched to the battle area was always recorded as over 80 per cent, displaying a rare unity of purpose and interest.

Both the United Nations and the European Community opposed Argentina's action in occupying the islands, but favoured long-term economic sanctions and diplomacy as the strategy for resolving the dispute. The USA, and later Peru, attempted diplomatic peace missions: 'Reagan yesterday launched a dramatic race against time to find a peaceful solution' (Roger Carroll, *Sun*, 8 April 1982). Those attempts did continue even as armed confrontation became closer. A month later the weekend media of 7–9 May were full of stories about attempted negotiations, and Argentinian intransigence, or stubbornness.

Britain pressed on with counter-invasion plans, despite the great difficulties created by being over seven thousand miles from the theatre of war, and in the face of some international opposition to military action. Although centrally involved in the peace attempts the US did give Britain material support: 'the degree of American help ... did make a difference'.[9] Nevertheless there was a strong sense of Britain going it alone, which is perhaps reflected in the national solidarity – although there were dissenting voices – shown in opinion polls. The jubilation and sense of triumph when British troops landed on the Falkland Islands, even though the war was far from over, was widespread, a typical headline declaring: 'OUR TROOPS GIVE 'EM HELL' (Brian Woosey and James Lawthwaite, *Sun*, 22 May 1982).

Although the result of the war may be considered a military success it was not an unmitigated, or total, triumph. Over 250 men of the British task force were killed, 6 ships and 34 aircraft were destroyed. Many more men were injured and vessels damaged, whilst Argentinian losses were even greater. The disasters were so profound that even the flag-waving tabloid press reported them in stark terms as Argentinian air attacks penetrated naval defences: 'OUR DARKEST HOUR' (George Lynn and David Kemp, *Sun*, 27 May 1982), and '70 DEAD' (Brian Woosey, *Sun*, 11 June 1982). There was great dismay, and a sense of unbelief at the news of these tragedies. Fortunately the war ended only four days after the second of these headlines, when the Argentinians surrendered.

The Belgrano Controversy

Apart from the question of whether or not the actual war could have been avoided, probably the most controversial episode in it was the sinking of the Argentinian cruiser *General Belgrano*. Britain had declared an exclusion zone of 200 miles around the Falkland Islands, and any Argentinian vessel entering that area was considered an aggressor. The *Belgrano* was sunk just outside the exclusion zone, and appeared to be returning to Argentina. The fact that 368 crew members were killed in the action intensified the controversy.

The immediate response of the *Sun* was triumphant: '*Our lads sink gunboat*' (Tony Snow, 4 May 1982). The report suggested it 'had been asking for trouble all day' by provocatively sailing in and out of the limit. There was a later accusation that the government knew the *Belgrano* was actually withdrawing from the conflict, and ordered its sinking for political rather than military reasons. Two years after the event a civil servant, Clive Ponting, with access to secret information, passed papers to a Labour MP implicating Thatcher in deception over the incident. Summarising the unresolved controversy Edgar Wilson has written:

> the British nuclear submarine *Conqueror*, [was] acting under instructions from the British War Cabinet. ... It is now clear that at the time the sinking was ordered, (1) the government knew of the Peruvian peace plan, (2) the Argentine ship was 59 miles outside of the 200 mile exclusion zone ... (3) ... was under orders to return to base, which fact was known to the British government, (4) ... that it was not a threat to the British task force. ... By sinking the *Belgrano* with great loss of life, the British government ensured a military solution was necessary, the successful outcome of which would reflect favourably on the New Right government. Not, however, if the British public knew of the circumstances.[10]

The government denied all these accusations at the time they were made, claiming that the final decision to torpedo the *Belgrano* had been taken in the war area, not in Britain. Thatcher later refuted the allegations, arguing: 'The decision to sink the *Belgrano* was taken for strictly military not political reasons. ... There was a clear military threat which we could not responsibly ignore.'[11] The use of 'we' perhaps suggests that it was a 'War Cabinet' decision, made collectively in Britain rather than in the theatre of war seven thousand miles away. Whilst regretting the loss of life, Thatcher disclaimed responsibility: 'The ship's poor state of battle readiness greatly increased the casualties.'[12] Whatever the truth of the matter, it does seem inconsistent to argue that the *Belgrano* was both 'a clear military threat' and in a 'poor state of battle readiness'.

The difficulty of interpreting historical 'facts' – the one (so far) undisputed factor is that the *Belgrano* was sunk by a British submarine – is further illustrated by taking into account the analysis of the political journalist Michael Charlton: 'Two hours before ... the Peruvian proposals were first talked over, the war Cabinet in London had given the Royal Navy permission to alter the rules of engagement, which authorized the sub-marine *Conqueror* to attack the *Belgrano*. Nothing was then known in London of the nature of Peru's involvement.'[13] Charlton argues from details of times, and this account also illustrates how crucial timing is during such a crisis, but precise times of events are not always easy to establish.

Sometimes the 'facts' of history can be challenged, and often, perhaps mainly, even when they can be established without doubt they need to be interpreted. This incident emphasises that history is not something simply to be 'learned' in an uncomplicated way, but has to be analysed, inter-preted, understood, often from different perspectives, or points of view.

Just to complicate matters a little further, in this case there is the later evidence of Admiral Gualter Allara, the Argentine naval commander of the area at the time, and in control of the *Belgrano's* movements when it was attacked by the *Conqueror*: 'from a strictly professional point of view, I cannot criticize that action. She [the *Belgrano*] was a ship carrying out a war mission. ... I do not criticize the British attack on a warship with a fighting capability, and on a military mission, when she was in the area of the conflict. ... That ship was in the area of operations.'[14] Whatever moral considerations are brought into account military strategy, tactics, appeared to be a factor in that terrible action. On this occasion it is difficult not to agree with Thatcher's judgement: 'The sinking of the *Belgrano* turned out to be one of the most decisive military actions of the war.'[15] From that day onwards the Argentine navy was kept away from the Islands, and that certainly aided the extremely hazardous task of actual invasion, and consequent victory.

2. GB, US and UN

The period covered by this book opened with a political argument about the extent to which Great Britain could be an independent military super-power:

MISSILE STORM IN COMMONS
£65m. BLUE STREAK ABANDONED
(*Financial Times*, 14 April 1960)

Britain simply could not afford to continue to develop extremely expen-sive high-technology weapons. Harold Watkinson, the Minister for

Defence, told the House of Commons: 'The technique of controlling ballistic missiles has rapidly advanced ... we ought not to continue to develop ... a missile that can be launched only from a fixed site ... our strategic nuclear force is an effective and significant contribution to the deterrent power of the free world. The Government do not intend to give up this independent contribution ... there appears much to be said for prolonging the effectiveness of V-bombers by buying supplies of the airborne ballistic missile Skybolt which is being developed in the United States' (*Hansard*, 13 April 1960).

This represented an uneasy compromise between having independence of use, and being reliant on the USA as the source of supply for missiles. The problem arose from the related twin factors of cost and the speed of technological development: 'The inevitable question which follows from this is whether in the present circumstances any one Western European nation is still in a position to solve these problems in isolation' (*Financial Times*, 14 April 1960). The European states were going to have either to develop a mutual defence system, or to be to some extent dependent on the US.

Since Britain and France, the latter being at the time the most powerful nation on mainland western Europe, were not especially friendly towards one another, Britain's interests were pushed westward. Less than three years later, in December 1962, this was confirmed when the British prime minister, Macmillan, accepted US Polaris missiles, although with the provision that Britain would supply the nuclear warheads. This again was a compromise. Britain's status was being upheld by having its own deterrent, but nevertheless she would be reliant on the USA in order to be able to use it. This simply reflected general European political reality at the time.

Throughout the 1960s Britain was receiving US economic aid, and whilst British governments discussed a withdrawal of military commitments from the Middle and Far East, nothing substantial was done. The Americans were keen that Britain should help to contain Communist expansion in areas such as Malaysia, and on the whole Britain did so. British attitudes may have been paradoxical. They wanted to give up some of the global responsibilities – Aldabra, a small island in the Indian Ocean, for example – but on issues such as the Southern Rhodesia crisis demanded freedom of independent action. British ambivalence was illustrated by official attitudes to the USA's involvement in Vietnam (basically a war the US had inherited from French imperialism). Britain refused direct participation in that war, but always supported the US diplomatically and in the United Nations. The deepening economic crises of the 1970s tended to restrain, or curtail, Britain's bids for independence of action in that decade.

The Libyan Crisis

Even after the almost solo action in the Falklands, which despite its cost was certainly considered a success, Britain remained closely linked to non-independent activity. This is illustrated by the international crisis of April 1986, when the USA launched air attacks against Libya because of that country's alleged involvement in international terrorism. The air strikes could not have been made without help from European countries, all but one of which opposed US policy in this case. However, the Thatcher government did allow the use of American air force bases in Britain and British Royal Air Force facilities in Cyprus, which caused considerable controversy. Even the pro-Thatcher *Daily Telegraph* (16 April 1986) reported that only Britain amongst the European NATO nations supported the US attack.

A more oppositional paper, the *Guardian*, on the same day expressed it in stronger terms, as Britain and the USA being alone in the world. Furthermore, it reported widespread unease amongst many Conservative MPs over Thatcher's support of Reagan's action. In fact the conservatively-inclined newspaper of this pair was honest enough to subsequently publish an opinion poll showing that 69 per cent of those questioned disagreed with the government's support of the US (*Daily Telegraph*, 17 April 1986).

To many people it looked as though Britain had simply followed US policy, either without thought or without real choice, adopting a role of dependency, or subservience. There was perhaps a half-hearted attempt in the *Daily Telegraph* of 16 April to argue that the USA was actually following Britain's earlier example in the Falklands, but that was not a generally accepted argument. The journalist Ian Waller summarised the situation differently: 'Far from raising the banner of "British pride", bombing Libya was seen as an act of submission to an irrational foreign power – the USA' (*New Statesman*, 25 April 1986). On the whole, Britain appeared to have lost the independence of action taken four years before.

The British government saw itself, although on that occasion apparently against the will of most Britons, acting in the best interests of the world as a whole, against international terrorism. It did so again in the crisis that erupted nearly five years later – but in 1991 Britain acted with the United Nations, rather than solely with the USA, and with the support of most Britons.

Desert Storm

In August 1990 Iraq invaded, and annexed, neighbouring Kuwait. The United Nations ordered a withdrawal, giving Iraq an ultimatum that failure to comply would result in military action. Almost six months later Iraq had strengthened its military position in Kuwait, and war seemed inevitable. Again there was criticism of British and American attitudes in the pacifically inclined press, with the *Guardian* (16 January 1991) in particular, reporting that the US and Britain had blocked a French peace-plan discussed at the United Nations.

The prime minister, John Major, had made the government's position clear the day before, in Parliament: 'We do not want a conflict. We are not thirsting for war, though if it comes I must say to the House I believe it would be a just war. ... What we cannot do is water down the existing Security Council resolutions which call for total and unconditional Iraqi withdrawal, or extend that UN deadline' (*Hansard*, 15 January 1991). Despite the *Guardian's* report of apparent isolation the operation was in fact truly international. The USA led it for obvious practical reasons, and Britain provided the greatest support, but it was a United Nations activity, and an example of Britain finding a role of global importance within a generally internationally approved framework.

Although there was dissent against the idea of war at all, there was also a contrary feeling that a limited operation to remove the Iraqi army from Kuwait would not be enough, a fear that UN troops involved in the operation known as Desert Storm would be prevented for political reasons from completing victory. These attitudes were typically expressed by one popular weekly newspaper: 'To stop the war and leave the tyrant and his threats in place would be military and political madness. ... The job of ending the power of Saddam Hussein has been well begun. It mustn't stop when it is only half finished' (*Sunday Mirror*, 20 January 1991). In order to bolster what it felt was a weakening of resolve, the paper's next edition carried the front-page headline: 'NEXT STOP BAGHDAD' (*Sunday Mirror*, 27 January 1991). That prophecy was not fulfilled, and subsequently Iraq's foreign policy behaviour, and the treatment of ethnic minorities within its borders, have been matters of recurring international concern. Britain, however, did centrally assist in achieving the implementation of the UN Security Council's resolutions.

3. B ... y Europeans

Britain's Conservative government originally applied to join the Common Market, as it was then popularly known, as early as 1961, but ran up against French opposition. The Labour Party opposed membership of the EEC (European Economic Community) at that time, but when in government, in 1967 renewed the application. The party in fact remained split on the issue, and there was little real momentum behind the policy. In the event, it was again vetoed by the French president, de Gaulle.

Early in the following decade, the 1970s, de Gaulle had departed and Heath, a very enthusiastic pro-European, had become Conservative prime minister of Britain. Even so, the matter was far from clear-cut. A survey conducted by the EEC itself in 1970 showed that 64 per cent of EEC citizens asked were in favour of British entry, and only 8 per cent against, the rest registering themselves as 'don't knows'. However, a mere 19 per cent of British people favoured membership, while 63 per cent opposed it. In presenting and commenting on these figures the political theorist Leslie Macfarlane has written: '[Opinion] Polls showed more persons opposing than favouring entry until the beginning of 1972 with opposition to entry increasing with age, and with lower socio-economic status, with women less favourably disposed to entry than men; Scotland and the North less than the South; and supporters of the Labour Party less than those of the Conservative and Liberal Parties. But ... there was no tight causal relationship between Party support and support for EEC entry.'[16] It was against this kind of confusing background that the government felt it had to begin to raise popular support for integration into Europe. It was also necessary to encourage enthusiasm amongst politicians.

Heath's own commitment as leader was very important, and that was reflected in a government White Paper – which served as both a document for consultation and a statement of intent – published in 1971. That document argued: 'Her Majesty's Government are convinced that our country will be more secure, our ability to maintain peace and promote development in the world greater, our economy stronger, and our industries and people more prosperous, if we join the European Communities than if we remain outside them.'[17] There was no doubting this government saw Britain's global role being exercised as part of Europe. It would not entail being a diminished, lesser power – but rather, operating in a different framework from the old imperial one.

It was necessary even for the government to win practical political support, for many Conservative, as well as Labour members, were against joining the EEC. A fear element was played on in terms of British power – if joining the EEC were rejected it would leave Britain in a political vacuum, unable to influence important events and policies:

> In a single generation we should have renounced an imperial past and rejected a European future. Our friends everywhere would be dismayed. They would rightly be as uncertain as ourselves about our future role and place in the world. Meanwhile the present Communities would continue to grow in strength and unity without us. Our power to influence the Communities would steadily diminish, while the Communities' power to affect our future would as steadily increase.[18]

Britain needed Europe more than Europe needed Britain, is the gist of the argument. That may, or may not, have been a harsh reality, but it is not necessarily a persuasive one. People may be persuaded to act in the way you want them to from fear, but they will not like doing so – and may indeed act oppositely in order to show they are not afraid.

Part of the persuasion was based on economics, always an important factor in political discussion: 'in 1958 average earnings in Britain were similar to those in France, Germany, Belgium and the Netherlands.... By 1969 earnings [in the EEC] ... were now between a quarter and a half higher on average than in Britain ... all the Community countries enjoyed rates of growth of gross national product (GNP) per head of population, or of private consumption per head, roughly twice as great as Britain's.'[19] Not only were the EEC countries, and the individuals in them, better off than Britain and the British, they were increasing the wealth gap, according to the White Paper. The document can be seen, perhaps, as an appeal to both fear and greed.

Agreement was reached at the European level of negotiations in 1972, but uncertainty remained in the British Parliament. Labour was still divided, and some Conservative MPs opposed entry into Europe. In a crucial House of Commons debate Enoch Powell articulated their perceptions in identifying what they saw as the consequences of Britain joining the EEC: 'this House and Parliament will lose their legislative supremacy ... legislative sovereignty, has to be given up ... this House loses its exclusive control ... over taxation and expenditure ... the judicial independence of this country has to be given up ... the law made elsewhere and the adjudication elsewhere will override the law which is made here ... consequently ... the self-government of the electorate is diminished' (*Hansard*, 17 February 1972). These were all issues still being debated twenty years later. Part of British reluctance to join Europe politically came from the feeling that it was giving up very many centuries of hard-won, and hard-kept, independence.

The balance was sufficiently delicate for Heath's Conservative government to be alarmed about the outcome of a parliamentary vote in which a number of backbench MPs, those without any special responsibilities in the government, were threatening not to support official policy:

Pressure on anti-Market Tories rises

The open war of nerves between the Government and its 'rebel' back-benchers . . . increased in tempo. . . . Several more potential 'rebels' were summoned to see the Prime Minister.

(Richard Evans, *Financial Times*, 17 February 1972)

Feelings were so strong even this tactic did not work, and some 'Tories' were willing to see their own party defeated rather than support entry into the EEC. Defeat in Parliament does not necessarily lead to a general election, but in this case the prime minister had declared that would be the result, as *The Times* of 18 February 1972 graphically recorded.

Ironically, even with this pressure, the government won the vote on the Bill, the formal proposal to join the EEC, only because Liberal Party MPs supported it. The media widely reported the scenes in the House of Commons following the vote, as some Labour MPs shouted verbal abuse at the Liberals, and even a degree of manhandling appeared to occur. Physical activity of that kind is rare, and the anti-Marketeers, those against closer political associations with Europe, clearly felt betrayed by people they felt should have been with them. It was, and to some extent has remained, a highly emotive issue.

That narrow government success enabled the procedure to go forward, and five months later the final House of Commons debate and vote on the matter was held. Peter Shore's speech expressing some Labour Party doubts dwelt on a mixture of economics and nationalism: 'the nation and the House has the sense that the broad effect of the treaty arrangements is damaging and that the enterprise is going wrong even before we have embarked upon it . . . with such a large European market looming, British industry is showing no signs of an imminent revival . . . [it] has become gloomier and gloomier in its view of future prospects. . . . We shall be forced to adjust the price of our food to bring our practices into line with those of the Continent . . . negotiations took place under the threat of a third French veto and we were allowed in only because the Prime Minister was brought to abandon every major British interest involved' (*Hansard*, 13

July 1972). Shore went on to speak of 'humiliation at the hands of France' (ibid.), another recurring idea over the subsequent decades, although in later years Germany also came to be seen as an EC ogre of Europe.

To some extent these fears are born of experience – the French did, for example, twice veto British entry in the 1960s, and therefore humiliate Britain. To some extent they are based on prejudice against 'bloody foreigners' in general. Geoffrey Rippon, speaking for the Government in the 1972 House of Commons debate, picked up the latter aspect: 'What the opponents of the Bill have principally in common is fear. They are dealers in fear: fear of foreigners, fear of change, fear of the unknown. . . . The building of a united Europe has been an objective of British foreign policy pursued by successive Governments for generations' (ibid.). It might be argued that the original impetus for European unity itself came from fear after 1945, fear of yet another war if nations were not bonded together in some formal manner. The question, however, was not about European unity, but Britain's relationship to it.

Also speaking for the Government, Geoffrey Howe went back to the argument and tone expressed in the previous year's White Paper:

> our country is taking this decisive step not in a mood of misery and mutual recrimination but in a mood of strength and confidence. . . . Europe is now faced with an opportunity of a great move forward in political unity and we . . . must play our part in it. . . . A decision to share power to the common advantage is an enhancement rather than a loss of sovereignty; and for so long as we remain a member of the Communities, pooling decisions in the interests of Europe as a whole rather than linking to the narrow interests of a single State, that, too, will be a deliberate and continuing exercise of national sovereignty. (ibid.)

Even with this impassioned plea the vote in the House of Commons was won by only seventeen, and that might have been much closer as 13 Labour MPs abstained. Had they voted against the Government, rather than showing their lack of support by simply not voting, abstaining, the actual majority in favour of joining the EEC would have been a mere four. It was an extremely close decision.

In and Out?

Britain formally joined the EEC on the first day of 1973, but the manner of its achievement inevitably meant the relationship would be uneasy. Just over a year later Heath was defeated in a general election, and the Labour Party coming to power in 1974 was committed to renegotiating the terms of Britain's EEC membership and putting them to a national referendum. This was unique in the British political system, which had always conceived democracy in terms of representatives. On this occasion everyone entitled to vote in an election had the opportunity to vote on the one issue: Britain's continued membership of, or withdrawal from, the EEC. In June 1975 the matter was settled with 67 per cent of electors voting for remaining within the Community. The number of votes cast was lower than in general elections, only 64 per cent of those entitled to cast an opinion actually doing so. Nevertheless it was a victory in favour of Europe.

Anti-Marketeers, however, continued to be unhappy about events. From their point of view the issues had not been presented honestly, and indeed the bias of the media was strongly in favour of remaining in Europe. In February most opinion polls showed a preference for rejection of staying in the EEC. Shortly before the referendum, however, polls were predicting – entirely accurately as it turned out – a 2 to 1 majority in favour of remaining in the Community. Commenting on that change the political analyst Professor Anthony King concluded (*Observer*, 1 June 1975) it had been caused by the messages in favour of the EEC coming from the leading politicians. Certainly, the tabloid popular press typically told its readers exactly what to do, and why:

Vote YES for Britain

If we leave now ... We shall be disregarded and dishonoured.
Vote Yes – and we shall at least have prospects: the prospect of friends and partners, the prospect of the power to direct and influence our own future – and the world's future.

(*Daily Mail*, 4 June 1975)

In the circumstances it is hardly surprising that the result of the referendum was greeted triumphantly: 'The United Kingdom proved ... and declared itself united' (David Cross, *Daily Mail*, 7 June 1975). Rippon's earlier argument that Britons 'fear change' seemed ironically a factor – when they were out they were afraid of going in, once they were in they were afraid of going out.

Not surprisingly in those conditions, there remained some unease. This re-surfaced later, over specific matters such as the Common Agricultural Policy – which many people in Europe felt the French used to their own advantage – and Britain's overall budget contributions to Europe. In addition, new factors arose in the following decade which again caused fundamental difficulties in the relationship of Britain and most of the other Community countries. One of these was the European desire for closer unity, including a common currency and a European Parliament that would supersede, override, the powers of national governments. Another was the rise to power of Thatcher, who was very suspicious of the ambitions of other European states. By the 1980s, although Heath continued to be a convinced European in Parliament he had no real political power; and of the two Labour leaders who had tried to get Britain into Europe in 1967 – Wilson and Callaghan – the former had retired and the latter had resigned from leadership of the Labour Party. It might be expected that in this new situation the eighties would be a troubled decade for relations between Britain and the now larger and more integrated EC (European Community).

Thatcher had become leader of the Conservatives, replacing Heath, in late 1975 and her attitude to Europe was much more suspicious than his. During the 1979 general election campaign one difference from previous campaigns had been signalled, with the *Daily Telegraph* (10 April 1979) in particular claiming that Europe had become a central issue. Within only a few months of gaining power Thatcher confronted Britain's partners over the question of contributions to the European budget – which was to become a recurring area of conflict. At the Dublin EEC summit in late November 1979 Thatcher fought a long battle that the *Daily Telegraph*, amongst other newspapers, reported as a great success, presenting Thatcher as a kind of folk hero, defending British interests against cunning and unscrupulous foreigners who were trying to humiliate and cheat Britain. *The Times* of 1 December 1979 reported Thatcher as issuing a warning to other EEC leaders, whilst the following day's *Sunday Times* saw her, apparently approvingly, as planning a war, metaphorically, against Europe. The Labour MP Tony Benn, however, was less impressed: 'Went in to hear Mrs Thatcher answer questions on the Dublin summit. She looked frightened – the first time I have seen her look like that. She had talked big about getting a billion back from the Common Market and it has backfired.'[20] This is another example of how history is as much a matter of perception as of facts. The one factor everyone agreed on was that Thatcher had set up, from the beginning of her period of power, an atmosphere of conflict, contention, in Britain's relations with the EEC.

Throughout the 1980s Thatcher was increasingly presented as confronting Europe in the defence of British interests. Arguments over budgets and funds recurred, but they became overshadowed as more countries joined the EC and plans for greater political integration progressed. A typical confrontation occurred towards the end of the decade when the prime minister made a speech, on 20 September 1988 to the College of Europe in Bruges, describing plans for more centralisation – 'a European super-state exercising a new dominance from Brussels'[21] – as a nightmare. Most reports interpreted it as very anti-European. However, a weekly journal commented on Thatcher's speech as a whole as being: 'a thoughtful, elegant essay on the Europe Britain would like to see . . . she showed a willingness to take the Community seriously and to accept that Britain's future is inextricably bound up with that of the EEC' (*The Economist*, 24 September 1988). The ambivalence, or uncertainty, reflected in the different interpretations to some extent summarises British attitudes to Europe. The traditional suspicion that 'b . . . y furriners' will try to cheat the British in some way, is countered by a feeling that, approaching the twenty-first century, Britain and Europe are inevitably one – that it is simply no longer possible to adopt the Victorian attitude that Britain alone rules the world.

That dichotomy, or duality, emerged embarrassingly for the government at the start of the 1990s when one of its ministers, Nicholas Ridley, was widely reported, slightly inaccurately, as having referred to bossy Germans and French poodles running Europe. The *Spectator* of 14 July 1990 carried the full text of Ridley's remarks, which were not so much an outburst against the idea of Europe as against Europeans. As such it expressed the dilemma of those politicians who saw unity as inevitable, but were suspicious of the motives of Britain's partners. Ridley's views were not, of course, well received by Britain's European partners, and he was forced to resign his place in the government. Somewhat paradoxically the effect of Ridley's indiscretion, by causing his resignation from office, moved the government more towards European unity, as the *Independent* (16 July 1990), especially, observed. The episode also made the government more cautious in its approach to the European issue, for it had revealed the danger of a split in the Conservative Party about the whole EC integration issue. Although there were many factors in Thatcher's fall from power, it is perhaps not insignificant that only four months after this diplomatic scandal she was removed from the leadership of the Conservative Party, and therefore as prime minister. A xenophobic prime minister may be an asset in the Falkland Islands, but is not necessarily so in Europe.

Nevertheless the Conservatives in Parliament did remain disunited. Although the controversial Maastricht Treaty, which provided for greater European integration on some matters, was eventually accepted by Parliament it had a rough passage. In a House of Commons vote on 8 March

1993 the government was defeated when forty-two rebels refused to support prime minister Major on the Treaty. Ultimately, however, when it was presented to them as a matter of government survival, the Treaty was ratified and came into operation eight months later.

Europe Disunited

In order to get a slightly wider perspective on Britain's metaphoric schizophrenia towards Europe – simultaneously wanting, and not wanting, to be part of it – it is helpful to remember that Europeans have had their differences of opinion with one another too. In 1992, for instance, the French referendum on the Maastricht Treaty gave the narrowest possible majority in its favour, 51 per cent against 49 per cent. The Danish people actually rejected the Treaty, and their government had to hold a second referendum in order to achieve the 'right' result with the aid of an enormous propaganda campaign. In the light of these two near-disasters it is not surprising that all other EC governments refused to allow their citizens an open vote on the issue.

There has also been fundamental uncertainty within the EC about some aspects of integration. One example is the attempt to create a single European currency and monetary system. An initial movement in that direction was the establishment in 1979 of the ERM (Exhange Rate Mechanism), in theory a system of controlling currency fluctuations so that member states could benefit from greater stability in exchange rates. Britain had a tortuous, even tortured, relationship with that framework. Thatcher's refusal to join it, against the wishes of her Chancellor of the Exchequer Nigel Lawson, caused his shock resignation in October 1989. Britain eventually joined the ERM in October 1990.

After the drama leading up to the decision, it surprised many people that, after only a short time, Britain left the ERM in September 1992. That episode was subsequently described, after he had been replaced, by the Chancellor of the Exchequer of the time, Norman Lamont, as humiliating for Britain. He also advised prime minister Major against any idea of Britain joining any future EC attempt to create formal monetary union. Lamont was quoted as holding the opinion: 'Given the right leadership, the British people could equal the best in the world' (interview with Trevor Kavanagh, *Sun*, 16 September 1993). His comments showed a disdain for Europe, a return to the Victorian idea of Britain going it alone, and can be interpreted as an attack on, and perhaps ultimately a challenge for, Major's leadership.

This is not, though, merely anti-European prejudice; there may be a

valid economic argument behind Lamont's attitude. In the same month
as Britain left the ERM, for instance, Italy did so too, and less than a year
later, in July 1993, the system itself dramatically collapsed within the EC.
With the French franc overvalued on the currency markets it was thought
that only a reduction in German interest rates could maintain its status,
and the Bundesbank was expected to take that action. In the event it did
not do so, and the whole ERM system disintegrated causing financial
chaos and confusion across the continent. The *Sunday Times* of 1 August
1993 unequivocally blamed the collapse on Germany for putting its own
domestic interests before those of European unity. The episode was
generally presented as one in which the theoretical vision of union had
come up against the reality of the essential self-interest of individual
states.

The European Community also failed to agree an integrated policy
towards the civil war that ensued with the break-up of the former state of
Yugoslavia. That it could not respond to a great, and politically threatening, tragedy occurring on its own borders was another argument used
by anti-EC people to illustrate that, ultimately, all the nations and governments put their own interests and electoral popularity before all other
considerations. The EEC/EC/EU is, of course, a creation of the mid,
and later, twentieth century. This is very recent in historical terms, and it
faces various forms of nationalism and suspicion that have existed for
many hundreds of years. Time will tell how it fares.

4. Britain's Other Friends

In the meantime the formal framework of the Commonwealth still exists
too. At the beginning of the period covered by this book the Commonwealth was going through a bad period. South Africa was expelled in 1961
– although readmitted in May 1994 – because of its apartheid policy,
amidst great ill-feeling, and later in that decade such episodes as the
Nigerian civil war and the Rhodesian crisis, which lasted through the
seventies, weakened the idea of unity of interests. Also, some of the newly
independent states, although officially remaining in the Commonwealth,
felt some antagonism towards Britain as a remnant of a recent imperial
past. As these problems gradually receded, and new generations of
post-colonial politicians began to take pragmatic, practical attitudes
towards Britain, for some commentators the concept of a Commonwealth unity of interests began, slowly, to re-emerge.

The 1993 Commonwealth Conference in Cyprus was attended, as the *Daily Telegraph* (21 October 1993) proudly reported, by the leaders of 40 governments from all over the world, representing many different races, colours and creeds. For at least one Conservative newspaper this represented hope for the future. It argued that the Commonwealth had a record of international problem solving, and could therefore replace the United Nations to some extent in acting as a positive and material force for peace. This may be seen as unduly optimistic; nevertheless, it can be argued that in the last decade of the century the United Nations has become engaged in an increasing number of operations, and however well-intended not all of them have been entirely successful. One reason for this expanded UN activity has been the ending of the US/USSR confrontation that dominated most of the period covered by this book. There is now, in some respects, more international cooperation, and that situation has existed only from the disintegration of the Soviet Union and the Communist Party in the late 1980s. On the other hand, new dangers to international peace have emerged that hardly existed in a serious form in 1960. Global politics are always changing, and therefore Britain's role cannot ever be static.

Notes

Introduction

1. *Nothing But the Best* (Anglo Amalgamated/Domino, 1964); director, Clive Donner; writer, Frederic Raphael.
2. Keith Middlemas, *Power, Competition and the State*, vol. II (Basingstoke: Macmillan, 1990) p. 9.
3. Ibid., p. 1.
4. Kenneth O. Morgan, *The People's Peace: British History, 1945–1989* (Oxford: Oxford University Press, 1990) p. 513.
5. David Dutton, *British Politics since 1945* (Oxford: Basil Blackwell, 1991) p. 68.

Chapter 1   Idealism and Reality

1. G. D. H. Cole and Raymond Postgate, *The Common People, 1746–1946* (London: Methuen, 1966) p. 544.
2. Charles Loch Mowatt, *Britain between the Wars 1918–1940* (London: Methuen, 1966) p. 1.
3. Sir William Beveridge, *Social Insurance and Allied Services* (London: His Majesty's Stationery Office, 1942) Cmd 6404, p. 6.
4. Pauline Gregg, *A Social and Economic History of Britain, 1746–1965* (London: Harrap, 1965) p. 449.
5. Kevin Jefferys, *The Attlee Government, 1945–1951* (London: Longman, 1992) p. 59.
6. W. N. Medlicott, *Contemporary England, 1914–1964* (London: Longman, 1967) p. 515.
7. David Dutton, *British Politics since 1945* (Oxford: Basil Blackwell, 1991) p. 39.
8. Ibid.
9. Jefferys, *The Attlee Government*, p. 49.
10. Arthur Marwick, *British Society since 1945* (Harmondsworth: Penguin, 1982) pp. 17–18.
11. Alan Sked and Chris Cook, *Post-War Britain* (Harmondsworth: Penguin, 1993) p. 103.
12. Kenneth Morgan, *The People's Peace: British History, 1945–1989* (Oxford: Oxford University Press, 1990) p. 181.
13. John Solomos, *Race and Racism in Contemporary Britain* (Basingstoke: Macmillan, 1989) p. 48.

14. John Osborne, *Look Back in Anger* (London: Faber and Faber, 1986) p. 9. All subsequent references are to this edition.

Chapter 2   'Money Makes the World Go Around'

1. *Cabaret* (ABC Pictures/Allied Artists, 1972); director, Bob Fosse; music/lyrics, John Kander, Fred Ebb; screenplay, Jay Presson Allen.
2. David Childs, *Britain since 1945* (London: Methuen, 1984) p. 140.
3. Reginald Bevins, *The Greasy Pole* (London: Hodder and Stoughton, 1965) p. 137.
4. Harold Macmillan, *At the End of the Day* (London: Macmillan, 1973) p. 92.
5. Kenneth Morgan, *The People's Peace: British History, 1945–1989* (Oxford: Oxford University Press, 1990) p. 214.
6. Ibid., p. 237.
7. Arthur Marwick, *British Society since 1945* (Harmondsworth: Penguin, 1982) p. 158.
8. Ibid.
9. Margaret Laing, *Edward Heath: Prime Minister* (London: Sidgwick & Jackson, 1972) p. 187.
10. Peter Sinclair, 'The Economy – a Study in Failure', in David McKie and Chris Cook (eds), *The Decade of Disillusion: British Politics in the Sixties* (London: Macmillan, 1972) p. 114.
11. Andrew Gamble, *Britain in Decline* (Basingstoke: Macmillan, 1990) pp. 22–3.
12. David Butler and Michael Pinto-Duschinsky, *The British General Election of 1970* (London: Macmillan, 1971) p. 61.
13. Ibid., p. 154.
14. Ibid., p. 156.
15. Ibid., p. 350.
16. Michael Nevin, *The Age of Illusions* (London: Victor Gollancz, 1983) pp. 59–60.
17. Ibid., p. 63.
18. David Dutton, *British Politics since 1945* (Oxford: Basil Blackwell, 1991) p. 68.
19. Alan Sked and Chris Cook, *Post-War Britain* (Harmondsworth: Penguin, 1993) p. 300.
20. Dennis Kavanagh and Peter Morris, *Consensus Politics from Attlee to Thatcher* (Oxford: Basil Blackwell, 1989) p. 42.
21. David W. Pearce (ed.), *Macmillan Dictionary of Modern Economics* (London: Macmillan, 1992) p. 232.
22. Denis Healey, *The Time of My Life* (London: Michael Joseph, 1989) p. 378.
23. Ibid., pp. 378–9.
24. Ibid., p. 383.
25. *Report of the Seventy-fifth Annual Conference of the Labour Party 1976* (London: The Labour Party, 1976) p. 188.
26. Ibid., p. 189.
27. Sir Keith Joseph, *Monetarism is Not Enough* (London: Centre for Policy Studies, 1976) p. 12.

28. *The Right Approach* (London: Conservative Central Office, 1976) p. 10.
29. Gamble, *Britain in Decline*, p. 148.
30. *The Right Approach*, p. 24.
31. *Conference of the Labour Party*, p. 189..
32. Sked and Cook, *Post-War Britain*, p. 322.
33. James Callaghan, *Time and Chance* (London: Collins, 1987) p. 528.
34. Clive Jenkins, *All Against the Collar* (London: Methuen, 1990) p. 144.
35. Tony Benn, *Conflicts of Interest: Diaries, 1977–80*, edited by Ruth Winstone (London: Arrow Books, 1990) p. 434.
36. Ibid.
37. Ibid., p. 435.
38. John Biffen, 'The Conservatism of Labour', in Maurice Cowling (ed.), *Conservative Essays* (London: Cassell, 1978) pp. 166–7.
39. Mary Loudon, *Revelations: The Clergy Questioned* (London: Hamish Hamilton, 1994) pp. 259–60.
40. Marwick, *British Society since 1945*, p. 284.
41. David Sanders, Hugh Ward and David Marsh (with Tony Fletcher), 'Government Popularity and the Falklands War: A Reassessment', *British Journal of Political Science*, vol. XVII (1987) p. 281.
42. Healey, *The Time of My Life*, p. 502.
43. Ibid.
44. Edgar Wilson, *A Very British Miracle* (London: Pluto Press, 1992) p. 93.
45. David Butler and Dennis Kavanagh, *The British General Election of 1987* (Basingstoke: Macmillan, 1988) p. 112.
46. Ibid., p. 118.
47. Peter Riddell, *The Thatcher Decade* (Oxford: Basil Blackwell, 1989) p. 211.
48. Alan Watkins, *A Conservative Coup* (London: Duckworth, 1992) p. 71.
49. Ibid., pp. 70–2.
50. Margaret Thatcher, *The Downing Street Years* (London: Harper Collins, 1993) pp. 839–40.
51. Ibid., p. 839.
52. David Butler and Dennis Kavanagh, *The British General Election of 1992* (Basingstoke: Macmillan, 1992) p. 252.
53. Ibid., p. 247.

Chapter 3 'Who Governs Britain?'

1. Alistair Michie and Simon Hoggart, *The Pact* (London: Quartet Books, 1978) p. 183.
2. David Owen, *Time to Declare* (London: Michael Joseph, 1991) p. 434.
3. Ibid., p. 443.
4. Ian Bradley, *Breaking the Mould?* (Oxford: Martin Robertson, 1981) p. 121.
5. Ibid., pp. 121–2.
6. Roger Levy, *Scottish Nationalism at the Crossroads* (Edinburgh: Scottish Academic Press, 1990) p. 58.
7. Billy Wolfe, *Scotland Lives* (Edinburgh: Reprographia, 1973) pp. 105–6.
8. Kenneth Morgan, *The People's Peace: British History, 1945–1989* (Oxford: Oxford University Press, 1990) p. 288.

9. L. J. Macfarlane, *Issues in British Politics since 1945* (London: Longman, 1986) p. 98.

10. Harold Jackson, 'Northern Ireland', in David McKie and Chris Cook (eds), *The Decade of Disillusion: British Politics in the Sixties* (London; Macmillan, 1972) p. 228.

11. Harold Wilson, *The Labour Government, 1964–1970: A Personal Record* (London: Weidenfeld and Nicolson, 1971) p. 693.

12. Ibid.

13. Andrew Roth, *Heath and the Heathmen* (London: Routledge & Kegan Paul, 1972) p. 232.

14. Norman Tebbit, *Upwardly Mobile* (London: Futura, 1989) p. 294.

15. David Waddington, *Contemporary Issues in Public Disorder* (London: Routledge, 1992) p. 158.

16. David Butler and Dennis Kavanagh, *The British General Election of February 1974* (London: Macmillan, 1974) p. 115.

17. Ibid., p. 273.

18. Barbara Castle, *The Castle Diaries, 1964–70* (London: Weidenfeld and Nicolson, 1984) pp. 560–1.

19. Ibid., pp. 690–1.

20. Peter Jenkins, *The Battle of Downing Street* (London: Charles Knight, 1970) p. 140.

21. Ibid.

22. Joe Gormley, *Battered Cherub* (London: Hamish Hamilton, 1982) p. 87.

23. Edgar Wilson, *A Very British Miracle* (London: Pluto Press, 1992) p. 94.

24. Ibid., p. 112.

25. Martin Holmes, *The First Thatcher Government, 1979–83* (Brighton: Harvester, 1985) pp. 34–5.

26. Geoffrey Goodman, *The Miners' Strike* (London: Pluto Press, 1985) p. 13.

27. Ibid., p. 17.

28. Peter Hain, *Political Strikes* (Harmondsworth: Penguin, 1986) p. 139.

29. Martin Adeney and John Lloyd, *The Miners' Strike, 1984–5: Loss without Limit* (London: Routledge & Kegan Paul, 1988) p. 42.

Chapter 4   Battles on the Streets

1. Alfred Willener, *The Action-Image of Society: On Cultural Politicization*, translated by A. M. Sheridan Smith (London: Tavistock Publications, 1970) p. x.

2. James Callaghan, *Time and Chance* (London: Collins, 1987) p. 258.

3. Martin Kettle and Lucy Hodges, *Uprising!* (London: Pan, 1982) p. 29.

4. Harris Joshua and Tina Wallace, *To Ride the Storm* (London: Heinemann, 1983) p. 210.

5. *The Scarman Report* (Harmondsworth: Penguin, 1982) p. 36.

6. Ibid., pp. 77–8.

7. Ibid., p. 199.

8. Joshua and Wallace, *To Ride the Storm*, p. 210.

9. John Benyon, 'Scarman and After', in John Benyon (ed.), *Scarman and After* (Oxford: Pergamon Press, 1984) p. 242.

10. Lord Scarman, 'An Epilogue', in ibid., p. 260.
11. *The Broadcaster Farm Inquiry* (London: Karia Press, 1986) p. xxii.
12. Alan Watkins, *A Conservative Coup* (London: Duckworth, 1992) p. 51.
13. David Waddington, *Contemporary Issues in Public Disorder* (London: Routledge, 1992) pp. 2–3.
14. Ibid., pp. 20–1.

Chapter 5   Battles for Minds

1. Keith Tompson, *Under Siege* (Harmondsworth: Penguin, 1988) p. 66.
2. A. W. Singham, 'Immigration and the Election', in D. E. Butler and Anthony King (eds), *The British General Election of 1964* (London: Macmillan, 1965) pp. 365–6.
3. Shamit Saggar, *Race and Politics in Britain* (London: Harvester, 1992) p. 107.
4. The full text of the speech is in Enoch Powell, *Reflections of a Statesman*, selected by Rex Collings (London: Bellew Publishing, 1991) pp. 373–9.
5. It has now passed into history in this corrupted form. Cf., as entirely random examples in authoritative books: Martin Barker, *The New Racism* (London: Junction Books, 1981) p. 38; Peter Brahan, Ali Rattansi and Richard Skellington (eds), *Racism and Antiracism: Inequalities, Opportunities and Policies* (London: Sage Publications, 1992) p. 18; John Solomos, *Race and Racism in Contemporary Britain* (Basingstoke; Macmillan, 1989) p. 91; Tompson, *Under Siege*, pp. xv and 65. Powell was actually quoting from Book 6 of Virgil's *Aeneid*.
6. Philip Rose (ed.), *Social Trends* (London: HMSO, 1993) pp. 15–16.
7. Nicholas Abercrombie, Alan Warde *et al.*, *Contemporary British Society* (Cambridge: Polity Press, 1992) p. 258.
8. Herman Ouseley, 'The Way Forward: Proposals and Prospects', in John Benyon and John Solomos (eds), *The Roots of Urban Unrest* (Oxford: Pergamon Press, 1987) p. 138.
9. Mary Eagleton (ed.), *Feminist Literary Criticism* (London: Longman, 1991) p. 135.
10. Arthur Marwick, *British Society since 1945* (Harmondsworth: Penguin, 1982) p. 150.
11. Germaine Greer, *The Female Eunuch* (London: Paladin, 1991) pp. 370–1.
12. Juliet Mitchell, *Women: The Longest Revolution* (London: Virago, 1984) p. 79.
13. Juliet Mitchell and Ann Oakley (eds), *What is Feminism?* (Oxford: Basil Blackwell, 1989) p. 2.
14. Abercrombie, Warde et al., *Contemporary British Society*, p. 206.
15. Margaret Laing, *Edward Heath: Prime Minister* (London: Sidgwick & Jackson, 1972) p. 2.
16. Rosalind Delmar, 'What is Feminism?', in Mitchell and Oakley, *What is Feminism?*, p. 1.
17. Cora Kaplan, 'Radical Feminism and Literature: Rethinking Millett's *Sexual Politics*', in Eagleton, *Feminist Literary Criticism*, p. 169.
18. Margaret Marshment, 'The Picture is Political', in Diane Richardson and Victoria Robinson (eds), *Introducing Women's Studies* (Basingstoke: Macmillan, 1993) p. 123.

Chapter 6 'b ... y furriners'

1. G. Jean-Aubrey, *Joseph Conrad: Life and Letters* (London: William Heinemann, 1927) p. 221.

2. Leslie Stone, 'Britain and the World', in David McKie and Chris Cook (eds), *The Decade of Disillusion: British Politics in the Sixties* (London: Macmillan, 1972) p. 122.

3. Joseph Frankel, *British Foreign Policy, 1945–1973* (London: Oxford University Press, 1975) p. 137.

4. Kenneth Morgan, *The People's Peace: British History 1945–1989* (Oxford: Oxford University Press, 1990) p. 407.

5. Ibid.

6. Lawrence Freedman, *Britain and the Falklands War* (Oxford: Basil Blackwell, 1988) p. 29.

7. Ibid., p. 94.

8. Ibid., p. 95.

9. Ibid., p. 72.

10. Edgar Wilson, *A Very British Miracle* (London: Pluto Press, 1992) p. 130.

11. Margaret Thatcher, *The Downing Street Years* (London: Harper Collins, 1993) p. 215.

12. Ibid.

13. Michael Charlton, *The Little Platoon* (Oxford: Basil Blackwell, 1989) p. 209.

14. Ibid., pp. 216–17.

15. Margaret Thatcher, *The Downing Street Years*, p. 215.

16. L. J. Macfarlane, *Issues in British Politics since 1945* (London: Longman, 1986) pp. 124–5.

17. *The United Kingdom and the European Communities* (London: Her Majesty's Stationery Office, 1971) Cmnd 4715, p. 2.

18. Ibid., p. 17.

19. Ibid., p. 15.

20. Tony Benn, *Conflicts of Interest: Diaries 1977–80*, edited by Ruth Winstone (London: Arrow, 1990) p. 561.

21. Alan Sked and Chris Cook, *Post-War Britain* (Harmondsworth; Penguin, 1993) p. 540.

Index